THE LAST DAYS

Michael E.B. Maher

Unless otherwise indicated, all Scripture quotations in this teaching are from the *New King James Version* of the bible.

2017

ISBN: 978-0-620-78232-6

Books by Michael E.B. Maher

Repentance from Dead Works
Faith Toward God
Doctrine of Baptisms
Laying on of Hands
Resurrection of the Dead
Eternal Judgement
Born Free from Sin
The Will of Man
The Conscience of Man
The Spirit of Man
The Mind of Man
The Body of Man
Spiritual Gifts
The Revelation Gifts
The Power Gifts
Ministry Gifts
There is Sin to Death
Prayer
Being led by the Spirit
Overcoming Unforgiveness
The Two Gospels Explained
Of Such is the Kingdom

Contents

Chapter 1

The early signs

Do not be deceived

Matthew 24:4 "And Jesus answered and said to them: "Take heed that no one deceives you."

The above scripture, records the opening statement made by our Lord Jesus, when He taught us on the subject, of the end times. It is important to note, that there is only area recorded in the bible, that the Lord warned us not to be deceived about, and that is the subject of the end times. The reason that our Lord warns us in this area, is because this is the one area, where the saints can more easily, be deceived. And I want you to also note, that the Lord places the onus on His saints, to ensure that they are not deceived. The reason He does this, is because He has given us more than enough signs to look for, relating to the end times, that will prevent us from being deceived. And so, in this book we will plainly list those end time events as revealed in scripture, so that no saint need be deceived, in these last days. Before the church age, many of the mysteries of God were hidden, but the moment the church was born, God began to reveal His mysteries to the saints, by His Holy Spirit (1 Corinthians 2:10). Part of the mysteries of God, are what will take place, in the latter days. It is not the will of God, that the church be ignorant, of latter day events. You will recall, that our Lord Jesus said that He no longer calls us servants, but rather His friends. For He said, that a servant does not know what His master is doing, but all things that He has heard from the Father, He has made known to us (John 15:15). The whole book of Revelation, was given by God to our Lord Jesus Christ, to show His church, events which must take place in the later days (Revelation 1:1). God certainly wants His children, to have full understanding, of the end times.

Acts 1:6-7 "Therefore, when they had come together, they asked Him, saying, "Lord, will You at this time restore the kingdom to Israel?" (7) And He said to them, "It is not for you to know times or seasons which the Father has put in His own authority."

So, what about the scripture quoted above, where our Lord tells us that it is not for us to know times or seasons, which our Father has put in His own authority? The Lord answered the disciples in this manner, in response to their wanting to know the exact date, that He would set up His kingdom on the earth. Although there are instances in scripture, when God has given exact times to His saints, this is not the norm. For example, God told Abraham exactly how many years the children of Israel would be in Egypt (Genesis 15:13). God also told the Jews, how long they would be in exile in Babylon (Jeremiah 29:10). But with regards to the end times, God has not given us knowledge of times or seasons. So, how are we to understand the end times, if it is not given to us to know times and seasons? Our Lord answered that question for us, when He taught us on the subject relating to the end times. For in His teaching, He revealed certain key events, that will take place in the later days. He then stated, that when we see these key events taking place, that we will know just how close we are, to the end of the age. In other words, we are to look for the key events that scripture reveals to us, and by them, we will know how close we are, to the end of the age.

Matthew 24:32-33 "Now learn this parable from the fig tree: When its branch has already become tender and puts forth leaves, you know that summer is near. (33) So, you also, when you see all these things, know that it is near--at the doors!"

In the above passage of scripture, our Lord used the analogy of a fig tree, putting forth it's leaves when summer is near, and by observing the fig tree, we know just how near, summer is. And so, there are certain key events revealed to us in scripture, that must take place prior to the second coming of our Lord Jesus Christ. In this book, I have listed some of those key events, in chronological sequence, so that it is easier for the believer, to understand the times in which they live. When our Lord Jesus returns to the earth, the church will be in one of two locations. There will be the saints who are in heaven, and there will be the saints who are on the earth. The saints that will be in heaven at that time, will be present with the Lord Jesus, when He descends to the earth.

1 Thessalonians 4:15-18 "For this we say to you by the word of the Lord, that we who are alive and remain until the coming of the Lord will by no means precede those who are asleep. (16) For the Lord Himself will descend from heaven with a shout, with the voice of an archangel, and with the trumpet of God. And the dead in Christ will rise first. (17) Then we who are alive and remain shall be caught up together with them in the clouds to meet the Lord in the air. And thus, we shall always be with the Lord. (18) Therefore comfort one another with these words."

In the above passage of scripture, the Holy Spirit refers to the dead in Christ rising first. All who are dead in Christ, are currently with Christ, in heaven. For the scripture teaches us that when the saints fall asleep, that they depart this life to be with the Lord Jesus in heaven (2 Corinthians 5:8). In the same passage quoted above, the Holy Spirit goes on to say that there will be saints alive on the earth, when our Lord Jesus returns to the earth. And so, clearly the church will be located in both heaven, and on the earth, when our Lord Jesus returns on that day. Because the saints in heaven, are currently with Christ, they will not be taken by surprise, at the return of the Lord. However, that will not be the case, for all the saints on the earth. The requirement for the saints on the earth, to not be taken by surprise at the Lord's return, is to watch.

Mark 13:35-37 "Watch therefore, for you do not know when the master of the house is coming--in the evening, at midnight, at the crowing of the rooster, or in the morning-- (36) lest, coming suddenly, he find you sleeping. (37) And what I say to you, I say to all: Watch!"

In Mark's gospel quoted above, our Lord Jesus admonishes us, to watch for His coming. The reason He tells us to watch, is so that we will not be found sleeping at His return. So, what are we to watch for? We are to watch the fig tree, to see if it's leaves have begun to show yet.

The early signs

1 Thessalonians 5:1-9 "But concerning the times and the seasons, brethren, you have no need that I should write to you. (2) For you yourselves know perfectly that the day of the Lord so comes as a thief in the night. (3) For when they say, "Peace and safety!" then sudden destruction comes upon them, as labor pains upon a pregnant woman. And they shall not escape. (4) But you, brethren, are not in darkness, so that this Day should overtake you as a thief. (5) You are all sons of light and sons of the day. We are not of the night nor of darkness. (6) Therefore, let us not sleep, as others do, but let us watch and be sober. (7) For those who sleep, sleep at night, and those who get drunk are drunk at night. (8) But let us who are of the day be sober, putting on the breastplate of faith and love, and as a helmet the hope of salvation. (9) For God did not appoint us to wrath, but to obtain salvation through our Lord Jesus Christ."

The Holy Spirit, in His letter to the church in Thessalonica, counsels the saints on the earth, to watch and be sober. For in the scripture quoted above, we see that the saints on the earth who watch and are sober, will not be taken by surprise when our Lord Jesus returns. In fact, the apostle Paul is so confident of the fact, that the church on the earth will be aware of the Lord's imminent return, that he says that he has no need to write to us concerning times and seasons. Conversely, it is just as clear that the saints who choose not to watch and be sober, will be taken by surprise, at the coming of the Lord Jesus. However, in that same passage of scripture, it is very plain to see, that the ones who will be clearly taken by surprise when the Lord returns, are all the unbelievers who will be dwelling on the earth at that time. For the scripture reveals to us that as far as the world is concerned, that they would have reached a stage where they could finally proclaim, that peace and safety had been attained in the earth. It will be in that instant, that sudden destruction will come upon them.

The fourth kingdom revealed

Daniel 7:2-12 "Daniel spoke, saying, "I saw in my vision by night, and behold, the four winds of heaven were stirring up the Great Sea. (3) And four great beasts came up from the sea, each different from the other. (4) The first was like a lion, and had eagle's wings. I watched till its wings were plucked off; and it was lifted up from the earth and made to stand on two feet like a man, and a man's heart was given to it. (5) "And suddenly another beast, a second, like a bear. It was raised up on one side, and had three ribs in its mouth between its teeth. And they said thus to it: 'Arise, devour much flesh!' (6) "After this I looked, and there was another, like a leopard, which had on its back four wings of a bird. The beast also had four heads, and dominion was given to it. (7) "After this I saw in the night visions, and behold, a fourth beast, dreadful and terrible, exceedingly strong. It had huge iron teeth; it was devouring, breaking in pieces, and trampling the residue with its feet. It was different from all the beasts that were before it, and it had ten horns. (8) I was considering the horns, and there was another horn, a little one, coming up among them, before whom three of the first horns were plucked out by the roots. And there, in this horn, were eyes like the eyes of a man, and a mouth speaking pompous words. (9) "I watched till thrones were put in place, And the Ancient of Days was seated; His garment was white as snow, And the hair of His head was like pure wool. His throne was a fiery flame, its wheels a burning fire; (10) A fiery stream issued and came forth from before Him. A thousand thousands ministered to Him; Ten thousand times ten thousand stood before Him. The court was seated, And the books were opened. (11) "I watched then because of the sound of the pompous words which the horn was speaking; I watched till the beast was slain, and its body destroyed and given to the burning flame. (12) As for the rest of the beasts, they had their dominion taken away, yet their lives were prolonged for a season and a time."

As I mentioned earlier, I have listed in chronological sequence, the key events that must take place before our Lord returns. God gave the prophet Daniel, several visions and dreams, relating to the end times. Our Lord would not have done that, if He did not want us to understand end time events, as they unfold. In fact, in teaching us on end time events, our Lord Jesus Himself, referred to one of Daniels' visions (Mark 13:14). The above passage of scripture, records one of the visions of the end times, as given to the prophet Daniel. In his vision, Daniel was shown four different beasts, and each beast represented a separate kingdom in the earth. That truth is revealed to us by the angel, when he explains the vision given to Daniel, in a later passage of scripture. In scripture, a kingdom refers to a grouping of nations that are allied to each other, in one way or another. From this passage of scripture, it is very clear that each of these kingdoms will be on the earth, when our Lord returns, for the vision links the four beasts to the day of judgement, as the court is seated, and the books are opened. And so, in the vision the Lord reveals to us, what will happen to each of those kingdoms, when He does return. He reveals that three of the kingdoms, will continue, after He returns to the earth. For the scripture says, that their lives will be prolonged for a season and a time. But, although the lives of these kingdoms will be prolonged for a period of time, the scripture reveals to us that their dominion will be taken away. In other words, although these kingdoms will remain on the earth when our Lord returns, they will no longer govern their own affairs. The reason they will no longer govern their own affairs, is because they will become subject to the rule and reign, of Jesus Christ. For our Lord Jesus will reign on the earth with His church, for one thousand years, when He returns to the earth (Revelation 20:4).

Psalms 48:1-8 "Great is the Lord, and greatly to be praised in the city of our God, In His holy mountain. (2) Beautiful in elevation, the joy of the whole earth, Is Mount Zion on the sides of the north, The city of the great King. (3) God is in her palaces; He is known as her refuge. (4) For behold, the kings assembled, they passed by together. (5) They saw it, and so they marveled; They were troubled, they hastened away. (6) Fear took hold of them there, and pain, as of a woman in birth pangs, (7) As when You break the ships of Tarshish with an east wind. (8) As we have heard, so we have seen in the city of the Lord of hosts, In the city of our God: God will establish it forever."

The early signs

The above passage of scripture, gives us an account of what it will be like on the earth, during our Lord's millennial reign. For the scripture reveals to us, that the kings of the unsaved nations of the earth, will be brought to the city of Jerusalem during that time, where they will be instructed by the Lord, and by His saints. Notice, that the scripture states that they will marvel at what they see, and that fear will take hold of them, when they see the glory of the Lord and of His saints, and the glory of the city of Jerusalem.

Psalms 72:5-15 "They shall fear You As long as the sun and moon endure, Throughout all generations. (6) He shall come down like rain upon the grass before mowing, like showers that water the earth. (7) In His days the righteous shall flourish, and abundance of peace, Until the moon is no more. (8) He shall have dominion also from sea to sea, And from the River to the ends of the earth. (9) Those who dwell in the wilderness will bow before Him, And His enemies will lick the dust. (10) The kings of Tarshish and of the isles Will bring presents; The kings of Sheba and Seba Will offer gifts. (11) Yes, all kings shall fall down before Him; All nations shall serve Him. (12) For He will deliver the needy when he cries, the poor also, and him who has no helper. (13) He will spare the poor and needy, and will save the souls of the needy. (14) He will redeem their life from oppression and violence; And precious shall be their blood in His sight. (15) And He shall live; And the gold of Sheba will be given to Him; Prayer also will be made for Him continually, and daily He shall be praised."

The early signs

The above passage of scripture, is another account of what it will be like, during our Lord's reign on the earth at that time. Again, we see the kings of the earth, bringing the Lord, presents and gifts, and in fear, falling down before Him, to worship Him. Notice also, that the scripture says that our Lord will reign, as long as the sun and moon endure. The reason it says that, is because at the end of our Lord's millennial reign, God the Father will create new heavens and a new earth, and our Lord Jesus will then deliver the kingdom to the Father, and they will reign together in the new Jerusalem (1 Corinthians 15:28). Scripture does not reveal too much detail, regarding the three kingdoms that will remain on the earth, when our Lord returns. Scripture does however, give us more insight into the fourth kingdom, described in Daniel's vision. The reason for that, is because it is the fourth kingdom, from which the Anti-Christ will emerge. For the Anti-Christ is the "little horn", referred to in Daniel's vision. And we see in the vision, that the "little horn", emerges from the fourth beast. If you study scripture, you will see that the fourth beast described in Daniel's vision, is very similar to the vision of the beast, that the apostle John saw, in the book of Revelation (Revelation, chapters 13 & 17). And the beast that the apostle John described in his vision, is a description of the Anti-Christ and his kingdom. Of the four kingdoms revealed in Daniel's vision, we see that it is the fourth kingdom, that will be destroyed by our Lord Jesus at His coming. For Daniel says, that he watched till the beast was slain, and its body destroyed, and given to the burning flame. So, whereas the other three kingdoms will remain on the earth, when our Lord returns, the kingdom of the fourth beast, will be destroyed. The reason that the fourth kingdom will be destroyed, is because this will be the kingdom, over which the Anti-Christ will reign. And so, the first key event that we see in scripture, that must take place before our Lord returns, is that this fourth kingdom must be made manifest in the earth.

Daniel 7:15-26 "I, Daniel, was grieved in my spirit within my body, and the visions of my head troubled me. (16) I came near to one of those who stood by, and asked him the truth of all this. So, he told me and made known to me the interpretation of these things: (17) 'Those great beasts, which are four, are four kings which arise out of the earth. (18) But the saints of the Most High shall receive the kingdom, and possess the kingdom forever, even forever and ever.' (19) "Then I wished to know the truth about the fourth beast, which was different from all the others, exceedingly dreadful, with its teeth of iron and its nails of bronze, which devoured, broke in pieces, and trampled the residue with its feet; (20) and the ten horns that were on its head, and the other horn which came up, before which three fell, namely, that horn which had eyes and a mouth which spoke pompous words, whose appearance was greater than his fellows. (21) "I was watching; and the same horn was making war against the saints, and prevailing against them, (22) until the Ancient of Days came, and a judgment was made in favor of the saints of the Most High, and the time came for the saints to possess the kingdom. (23) "Thus, he said: 'The fourth beast shall be A fourth kingdom on earth, which shall be different from all other kingdoms, and shall devour the whole earth, trample it and break it in pieces. (24) The ten horns are ten kings Who shall arise from this kingdom. And another shall rise after them; He shall be different from the first ones, and shall subdue three kings. (25) He shall speak pompous words against the Most High, Shall persecute the saints of the Most High, And shall intend to change times and law. Then the saints shall be given into his hand for a time and times and half a time. (26) 'But the court shall be seated, and they shall take away his dominion, to consume and destroy it forever."

This second passage of scripture that we have looked at, is the explanation given to Daniel, of the vision that he saw. There are several things revealed to us from this passage of scripture, and by looking at the explanation given, we can better understand this fourth kingdom, from which the Anti-Christ will arise. From the angel's explanation, we clearly understand that there are ten kings, that will arise to reign over this fourth kingdom. And of those ten kings, three will be subdued by the Anti-Christ, when he emerges to take full control of the fourth kingdom. We also see that the Anti-Christ, will persecute the saints residing on the earth at that time. For the scripture says that he was able to make war against the saints, and prevail against them. We also see that the saints will experience his reign on the earth, for a period of three and a half years. For again the scripture says, that the saints shall be given into his hand, for a time and times and half a time. This account agrees with the book of Revelation, which states that the Anti-Christ will reign for a period of forty-two months (Revelation 13:5). In Daniel's vision, he tells us that the fourth beast was different from all the other beasts, and the angel also confirms, that the fourth kingdom will be different to all other kingdoms. I want you to notice that this kingdom, will not only be different to the three kingdoms that will be on the earth at that time, but the scripture also reveals to us that this kingdom will be different from all kingdoms that came before it, as well. The reason, that this kingdom will be different to all other kingdoms, is because all kingdoms that have ever arisen in the earth, have been secular in nature. This fourth kingdom however, will be a kingdom based on religion first, and secular power second. We will see this truth more clearly, as we examine scripture further. Because the ten kings and the Anti-Christ, will emerge out of this fourth kingdom, we see clearly that this fourth kingdom must be in place before the ten kings, and the Anti-Christ can be manifested. As we examine scripture further, we shall see that this fourth kingdom, is already in the earth today.

Daniel 8:1-26 "In the third year of the reign of King Belshazzar a vision appeared to me--to me, Daniel--after the one that appeared to me the first time. (2) I saw in the vision, and it so happened while I was looking, that I was in Shushan, the citadel, which is in the province of Elam; and I saw in the vision that I was by the River Ulai. (3) Then I lifted my eyes and saw, and there, standing beside the river, was a ram which had two horns, and the two horns were high; but one was higher than the other, and the higher one came up last. (4) I saw the ram pushing westward, northward, and southward, so that no animal could withstand him; nor was there any that could deliver from his hand, but he did according to his will and became great. (5) And as I was considering, suddenly a male goat came from the west, across the surface of the whole earth, without touching the ground; and the goat had a notable horn between his eyes. (6) Then he came to the ram that had two horns, which I had seen standing beside the river, and ran at him with furious power. (7) And I saw him confronting the ram; he was moved with rage against him, attacked the ram, and broke his two horns. There was no power in the ram to withstand him, but he cast him down to the ground and trampled him; and there was no one that could deliver the ram from his hand. (8) Therefore, the male goat grew very great; but when he became strong, the large horn was broken, and in place of it four notable ones came up toward the four winds of heaven. (9) And out of one of them came a little horn which grew exceedingly great toward the south, toward the east, and toward the Glorious Land. (10) And it grew up to the host of heaven; and it cast down some of the host and some of the stars to the ground, and trampled them. (11) He even exalted himself as high as the Prince of the host; and by him the daily sacrifices were taken away, and the place of His sanctuary was cast down. (12) Because of transgression, an army was given over to the horn to oppose the daily sacrifices; and he cast truth down to the ground. He did all this and prospered. (13) Then I heard a holy one speaking; and another holy one said to that certain one who was speaking, "How long will the vision be, concerning the daily sacrifices and the transgression of desolation, the giving of both the sanctuary and the host to be trampled underfoot?" (14) And he said to me, "For two thousand three hundred days; then the sanctuary shall be cleansed." (15) Then it happened, when I, Daniel, had seen the vision and was seeking the meaning, that suddenly there stood before me one having the appearance of a man. (16) And I heard a man's voice between the banks of the Ulai, who called, and said, "Gabriel, make this man understand the vision." (17) So, he came near where I stood, and when he came I was afraid and fell on my face; but he said to me, "Understand, son of man, that the vision refers to the time of the end." (18) Now, as he was speaking with me, I was in a deep sleep with my face to the ground; but he touched me, and stood me upright. (19) And he said, "Look, I am making known to you what shall happen in the latter time of the indignation; for at the appointed time the end shall be. (20) The ram which you saw, having the two horns--they are the kings of Media and Persia. (21) And the male goat is the kingdom of Greece. The large horn that is between its eyes is the first king. (22) As for the broken horn and the four that stood up in its place, four kingdoms shall arise out of that nation, but not with its power. (23) "And in the latter time of their kingdom, When the transgressors have reached their fullness, A king shall arise, having fierce features, who understands sinister schemes. (24) His power shall be mighty, but not by his own power; He shall destroy fearfully, And shall prosper and thrive; He shall destroy the mighty, and also the holy people. (25) "Through his cunning He shall cause deceit to prosper under his rule; And he shall exalt himself in his heart. He shall destroy many in their prosperity. He shall even rise against the Prince of princes; But he shall be broken without human means. (26) "And the vision of the evenings and mornings Which was told is true;

The early signs

Therefore, seal up the vision, for it refers to many days in the future."

In this second vision given to the prophet Daniel, relating to the end times, the Lord gives us some more insight, regarding the Anti-Christ. More specifically, this vision reveals to us the geographic location, of his kingdom. This vision, is linked to the earlier vision that we have already discussed, as Daniel mentions that this vision was given to him, after the first one that he had received. There are three main aspects to this vision. The first aspect, relates to the empires of Media and Persia, that would arise from within the Babylonian empire, which existed at the time that Daniel received his vision, and their subsequent destruction by the Greek empire, under Alexander the Great. For the angel explains the vision to us, by telling us that, "the ram which you saw, having the two horns--they are the kings of Media and Persia. And the male goat is the kingdom of Greece. The large horn that is between its eyes is the first king. As for the broken horn and the four that stood up in its place, four kingdoms shall arise out of that nation, but not with its power." That aspect of this vision, referred to future events, when Daniel received it, but that aspect is now historical for us, because we have seen it come to pass. For historical accounts, have shown us that the Median empire succeeded the Babylonian empire, and that the Persian empire, then replaced the Median empire. History went on to show us, that the Grecian empire, under Alexander the Great, replaced the Persian empire. Alexander the Great, was the "large horn", mentioned by the angel in this vision. Below, is a map showing the extent of Alexander the Great's, empire. The preceding Persian, Median and Babylonian empires, all fell within the geographic borders of Alexander's empire, but never reached to the same extent as his empire. Nevertheless, all four empires, were centred on the ancient city of Babylon.

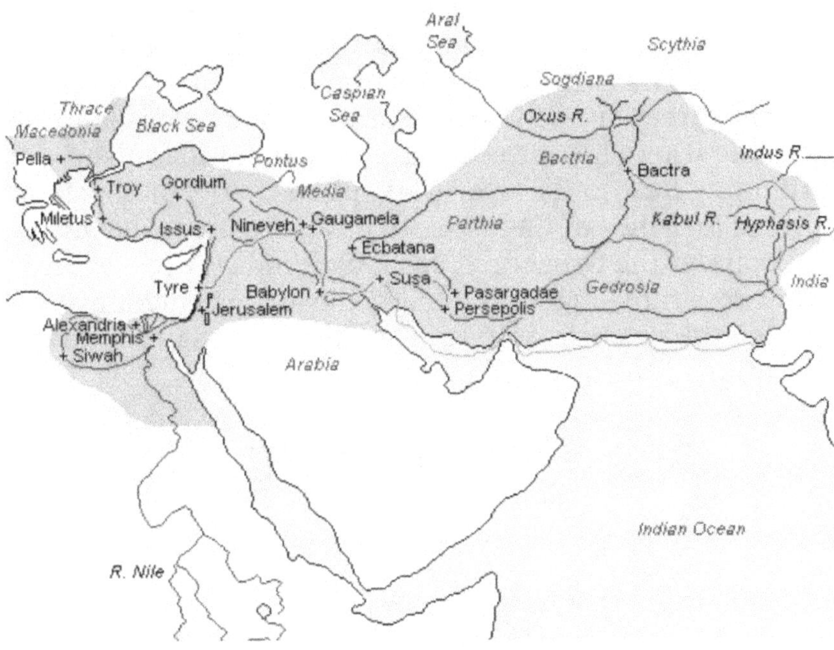

And then finally, history reveals to us that when Alexander the Great died, that his empire was split up into four separate kingdoms. As we will see, it is from one of these kingdoms, that the Anti-Christ will arise, in the last days. One of the reasons that the Lord put that aspect into this vision, was so that we would be able to clearly identify, the geographic location of the Anti-Christ's kingdom. And so, the second aspect of the vision, relates to the geographic location of the vision itself. The third aspect of the vision, refers to the rise of the Anti-Christ himself, and the rise of his kingdom. We have already looked at the part of the vision, that for us today, is historical. So, let us now look at the second aspect of the vision, which we have said is the geographical aspect. Notice, that our Lord placed Daniel in a very specific geographic point, when He gave him this vision. When he received the vision, Daniel was not physically at that location. The Holy Spirit took him there in the vision, and by the direction of the Holy Spirit, Daniel recorded for us, exactly where he was standing. Daniel found himself standing next to the river Ulai, in the citadel of Shushan, in the province of Elam. As we have already seen, when Alexander the Great died, his kingdom was divided into four separate kingdoms. One of those four kingdoms, was called the Seleucid empire. The following map shows the location of the Seleucid empire.

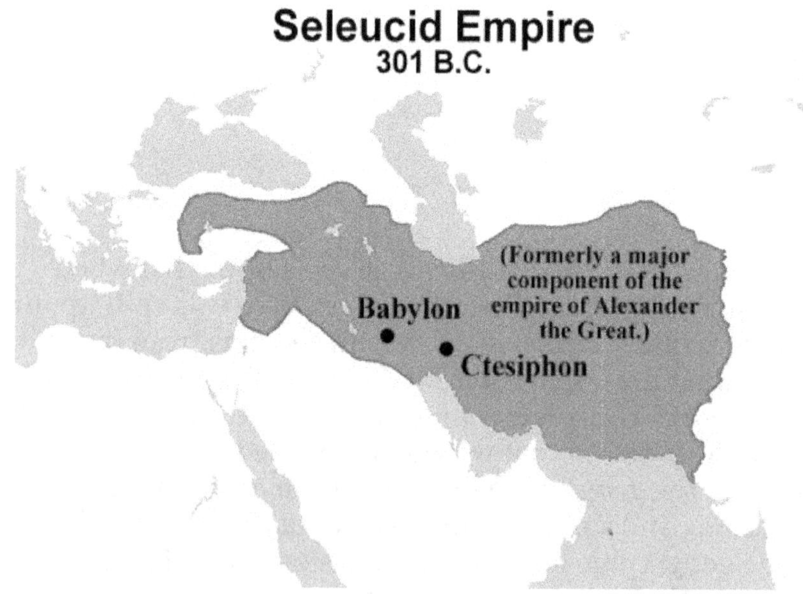

The early signs

The Seleucid empire was located geographically, in the same place, where Daniel was standing when he received his vision. In his vision, the angel Gabriel, revealed to Daniel that the kingdom of the Anti-Christ, would arise from that geographic location, in the last days. For in the vision, the Lord revealed to Daniel, that the kingdom of the "little horn", which represented the kingdom of the Anti-Christ, would grow exceedingly great, from that geographic point. The Lord showed Daniel, that the kingdom of the Anti-Christ would from that point, grow exceedingly great toward the south, toward the east, and toward the Glorious Land. The Glorious Land in this vision, refers to the land of Israel. If we were to stand today, at the same geographic point, that Daniel was standing at when he received his vision, we would be standing in what is today, modern-day Iran. The following map highlights the point where Daniel was standing when he received his vision.

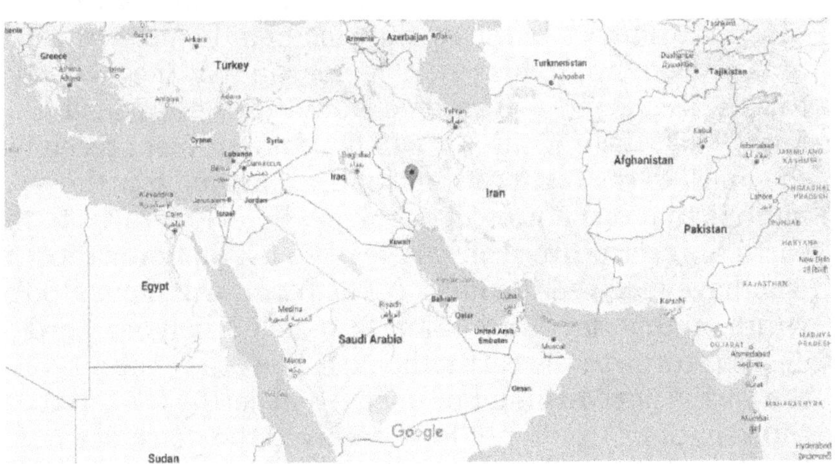

The early signs

To the south of that position today, we have Saudi Arabia and the whole Arabian Peninsula. To the east of that position today, we have Iran, Afghanistan and Pakistan. And towards the Glorious Land (Israel) from that position today, we have Iraq, Syria, Jordon, Lebanon, Egypt and Turkey. These countries today, are almost all, one hundred percent Muslim nations, except for Lebanon which still has a large Christian population, but nevertheless, the majority in that nation, are Muslims. There are other smaller nations, in the immediate vicinity, which are also all Muslim nations, but I have listed just the main ones. Clearly, the fourth kingdom is already in place, and awaiting the manifestation of the ten kings (leaders), who will in turn submit their authority to the Anti-Christ, who also will arise from among them. The fourth kingdom, is what we know today, as Islam. And so, we see that the reason the fourth kingdom is different from all other kingdoms, is because it is firstly, a kingdom of religion, and secondly, it is a kingdom of secular power. When the Anti-Christ is finally revealed in the earth, all Muslim countries in the earth, will align themselves with him, and submit to his rule. The reason that they will do this, is because he will emerge from within the Muslim faith. The Muslim nations, will have no problem receiving the mark of the beast as they follow him, and it is those nations that our Lord will destroy, when He returns to the earth. For scripture clearly reveals to us, that only those who have received the mark of the beast, will incur God's wrath on that day (Revelation 14:9-10). When our Lord Jesus returns to the earth, there will be other nations on the earth (not Muslim, but unsaved nevertheless), and those nations would not have received the mark of the beast, or followed him. And so, those nations will not be destroyed, when our Lord returns. You will recall that in

The early signs

Daniel's earlier vision that we looked at, that our Lord showed him that four kingdoms will be on the earth, when our Lord returns, and that it is the fourth kingdom that will be destroyed, while the other three remain. The other three kingdoms will all consist of nations of unbelievers, and it is these nations that our Lord Jesus and His saints will reign over, during His thousand-year reign on the earth. The fourth kingdom is already in place, which is the Muslim faith. Scripture reveals to us, that the ten kings and the Anti-Christ, will arise from this kingdom. The extent of reach, of the fourth kingdom in the earth, has not yet been revealed. But currently, Islam is growing faster than any other religion. And at the current growth rate, it is estimated that by the year 2030, Muslims will make up more than one quarter, of the world's population.[1]

I will close off this section, by recounting a dream that the Lord gave to me in 2014. In my dream, I found myself talking to a Muslim woman. As I spoke to her, the Lord revealed to me that she used to be one of His children. I questioned her about this, and she said that she no longer followed Jesus. I knew by the revelation of the Holy Spirit, that she had once been born again, filled with the Spirit, and had operated in the gifts of the Spirit. I also knew that she had been a Christian for several years. When I realized that she was now lost for all eternity, because she had turned her back on Jesus, I wept. Because I knew that she could no longer come back to Jesus, I told her that because of what she had done, that Jesus would never take her back. This did not seem to bother her at all. In my dream, she then disappeared, and I found a young man standing in front of me. This man had also accepted the Muslim faith, and he too had been a Christian at one time. When I questioned him about this, he also informed me that he too had once been born again, filled with the Spirit, and operated in the gifts of the Spirit, and he had been taught God's word. I was shocked to hear what he told me. I then told him that because of his denying the Lord Jesus, and accepting another faith, that he would suffer eternal damnation. He too, was not in the least bit bothered with what I said. I then said to someone who was with me (I do not know who this person was) that this must be the last days, because in just one day, I had now met two people who had fallen away from following Jesus, as their Lord and Saviour. I then looked off to one side, and there stood four believers in the Lord. They were mocking these two, who had denied their faith in Jesus. In my dream, I walked up to them and said to them that they should not mock, but rather fear. Because if the Lord had rejected these who had denied Him, it was only by His grace that they were His children. My dream ended there. As I have already stated, the Lord gave me this dream in 2014. Although I did not understand the full significance at the time, I knew that there must be some significance in that both individuals in my dream, had accepted the Muslim faith. It was only in the early part of 2016 however, that the Lord gave me understanding in the two visions that Daniel had, and how they relate to the fourth kingdom being the Muslim faith. The bible talks of a time when the whole world will marvel and follow the beast. It is not impossible, that some Christians will be deceived into following him in that day. We must all be vigilant in these last days, for our Lord told us to see that we are not deceived. The onus is on us to prevent that from happening. But the point remains clear, that the first of the key events has already happened. The fourth kingdom has already been manifested in the earth.

The seven kings revealed

Revelation 17:1-11 "Then one of the seven angels who had the seven bowls came and talked with me, saying to me, "Come, I will show you the judgment of the great harlot who sits on many waters, (2) with whom the kings of the earth committed fornication, and the inhabitants of the earth were made drunk with the wine of her fornication." (3) So, he carried me away in the Spirit into the wilderness. And I saw a woman sitting on a scarlet beast which was full of names of blasphemy, having seven heads and ten horns. (4) The woman was arrayed in purple and scarlet, and adorned with gold and precious stones and pearls, having in her hand a golden cup full of abominations and the filthiness of her fornication. (5) And on her forehead a name was written: Mystery, Babylon the Great, the mother of harlots, and of the abominations of the earth. (6) I saw the woman, drunk with the blood of the saints and with the blood of the martyrs of Jesus. And when I saw her, I marveled with great amazement. (7) But the angel said to me, "Why did you marvel? I will tell you the mystery of the woman and of the beast that carries her, which has the seven heads and the ten horns. (8) The beast that you saw was, and is not, and will ascend out of the bottomless pit and go to perdition. And those who dwell on the earth will marvel, whose names are not written in the Book of Life from the foundation of the world, when they see the beast that was, and is not, and yet is. (9) "Here is the mind which has wisdom: The seven heads are seven mountains on which the woman sits. (10) There are also seven kings. Five have fallen, one is, and the other has not yet come. And when he comes, he must continue a short time. (11) The beast that was, and is not, is himself also the eighth, and is of the seven, and is going to perdition."

The Lord reveals several things pertaining to the end times, in the above passage of scripture. The beast in this passage, refers to the Anti-Christ. We will discuss the Anti-Christ, Great Babylon the harlot, and the ten horns, later in this teaching, but in this section, we want to concentrate on the seven heads of the beast, as seen by the apostle John. In explaining the mystery of the beast to us, the angel refers to the seven heads of the beast, as seven mountains, and also as seven kings. In scripture, mountains very often refer to kingdoms.

Isaiah 2:2 "Now it shall come to pass in the latter days That the mountain of the Lord's house Shall be established on the top of the mountains, and shall be exalted above the hills; And all nations shall flow to it."

For example, in the above passage of scripture, the mountains mentioned, refer to the Lord's kingdom and the kingdoms of the earth. And the hills mentioned in this passage, refer to the nations of the earth. And so, it would not do the passage an injustice, to record it in the following manner, "Now it shall come to pass in the latter days that the kingdom of the Lord's house shall be established on top of the kingdoms, and shall be exalted above the nations; And all nations shall flow to it". In that light, and the fact that the angel has told us, that the seven mountains are also seven kings, we can confidently interpret the seven heads of the beast, to represent seven kingdoms. And so, because we know that the angel was speaking about seven kingdoms, the information given to us by the angel, makes it that much clearer for us to identify which kingdoms he was referring to. For the angel tells us, that at the time that the apostle John was given the vision, that five of those kingdoms had already ceased to exist, that the sixth kingdom was still in place, and that the seventh kingdom had not yet been manifested. So how do we establish which kingdoms, the angel was referring to? There are three keys in this vision, that help us to identify which kingdoms the angel was referring to. The first is Babylon. The second are the ten horns. And the third is the beast himself. In this section, we are looking primarily at the vision of the end times, as given to the apostle John. In the previous section, we looked primarily, at the visions of the end times, given to the prophet Daniel. Both Daniel's and John's visions of the end times, are very closely linked. For both Daniel and John, were given visions of the Anti-Christ. Both Daniel and John, were also shown the ten kings, that would arise in the last days. In Daniel's visions, we have already seen that these ten kings and the Anti-Christ, would arise from the geographic region, of the ancient kingdom of Babylon. And as we study John's vision, specifically relating to the seven heads of the beast, or the seven kingdoms, we will see that the geographic region of the ancient kingdom of Babylon, also features in his vision. And so, for us to more clearly understand which kingdoms the angel was referring to in John's vision, we need to go back, and look at the dream of the end times, that God gave to Nebuchadnezzar, the king of the Babylonian empire, and Daniel's interpretation of that dream.

The early signs

Daniel 2:27-45 "Daniel answered in the presence of the king, and said, "The secret which the king has demanded, the wise men, the astrologers, the magicians, and the soothsayers cannot declare to the king. (28) But there is a God in heaven who reveals secrets, and He has made known to King Nebuchadnezzar what will be in the latter days. Your dream, and the visions of your head upon your bed, were these: (29) As for you, O king, thoughts came to your mind while on your bed, about what would come to pass after this; and He who reveals secrets has made known to you what will be. (30) But as for me, this secret has not been revealed to me because I have more wisdom than anyone living, but for our sakes who make known the interpretation to the king, and that you may know the thoughts of your heart. (31) "You, O king, were watching; and behold, a great image! This great image, whose splendor was excellent, stood before you; and its form was awesome. (32) This image's head was of fine gold, its chest and arms of silver, its belly and thighs of bronze, (33) its legs of iron, its feet partly of iron and partly of clay. (34) You watched while a stone was cut out without hands, which struck the image on its feet of iron and clay, and broke them in pieces. (35) Then the iron, the clay, the bronze, the silver, and the gold were crushed together, and became like chaff from the summer threshing floors; the wind carried them away so that no trace of them was found. And the stone that struck the image became a great mountain and filled the whole earth. (36) "This is the dream. Now we will tell the interpretation of it before the king. (37) You, O king, are a king of kings. For the God of heaven has given you a kingdom, power, strength, and glory; (38) and wherever the children of men dwell, or the beasts of the field and the birds of the heaven, He has given them into your hand, and has made you ruler over them all--you are this head of gold. (39) But after you shall arise another kingdom inferior to yours; then another, a third kingdom of bronze, which shall rule over all the earth. (40) And the fourth kingdom shall be as strong as iron, inasmuch as iron breaks in pieces and shatters everything; and like iron that crushes, that kingdom will break in pieces and crush all the others. (41) Whereas you saw the feet and toes, partly of potter's clay and partly of iron, the kingdom shall be divided; yet the strength of the iron shall be in it, just as you saw the iron mixed with ceramic clay. (42) And as the toes of the feet were partly of iron and partly of clay, so the kingdom shall be partly strong and partly fragile. (43) As you saw iron mixed with ceramic clay, they will mingle with the seed of men; but they will not adhere to one another, just as iron does not mix with clay. (44) And in the days of these kings the God of heaven will set up a kingdom which shall never be destroyed; and the kingdom shall not be left to other people; it shall break in pieces and consume all these kingdoms, and it shall stand forever. (45) Inasmuch as you saw that the stone was cut out of the mountain without hands, and that it broke in pieces the iron, the bronze, the clay, the silver, and the gold--the great God has made known to the king what will come to pass after this. The dream is certain, and its interpretation is sure."

As we examine scripture, we will see that the seven kingdoms referred to in John's vision, all centred around the city of Babylon, which is why God gave the above dream of the end times, to the king of Babylon. In other words, God's prophetic timeline so to speak, for both Daniel's and John's visions, began with the Babylonian empire. And so, in that light, we see that the first of the seven kingdoms, mentioned by the angel in John's vision, is the same first kingdom as revealed in Nebuchadnezzar's dream, i.e. the Babylonian empire (the head of gold). The second of the seven kingdoms mentioned by the angel, refers to the second kingdom as revealed in Nebuchadnezzar's dream, i.e. the Median empire (the chest and arms of silver), which succeeded the Babylonian empire. The third of the seven kingdoms mentioned by the angel, refers to the third kingdom as revealed in Nebuchadnezzar's dream, i.e. the Persian empire (the belly and thighs of bronze), which succeeded the Median empire. The fourth of the seven kingdoms mentioned by the angel, refers to the fourth kingdom as revealed in Nebuchadnezzar's dream, i.e. the Grecian empire (the legs of iron), which succeeded the Persian empire. These four kingdoms, are also clearly listed for us in Daniel's visions that we have looked at in the previous section (Daniel 7 & 8). And in all four of these kingdoms, the city of Babylon, featured as a focal point, including the Grecian empire, for it was in the city of Babylon, that the ruler of that empire, Alexander the Great, died. Bearing in mind, that because all seven kingdoms mentioned by the angel in John's vision, are linked to the city of Babylon, the fifth of the seven kingdoms, would then have been the Seleucid empire, which succeeded the Grecian empire. For the Seleucid empire, also controlled the city of Babylon. You will recall, that we have already seen how the Seleucid empire relates to end time events, in the previous section. By the time that John received his vision from the Lord, the Seleucid empire no longer existed. And so, as stated by the angel, we see that five of the seven kingdoms, had fallen by that time. The kingdom that replaced the Seleucid empire, was the Parthian empire, and that empire also encompassed the city of Babylon. However, by that time, the city of Babylon had begun to decline quite dramatically in stature, but nevertheless the city remained. It was the Parthian empire, that was in existence when John received his vision, and this sixth empire, is the kingdom that the angel referred to, as being present on the earth, at that time. Below is a map showing the extent of the Parthian empire.

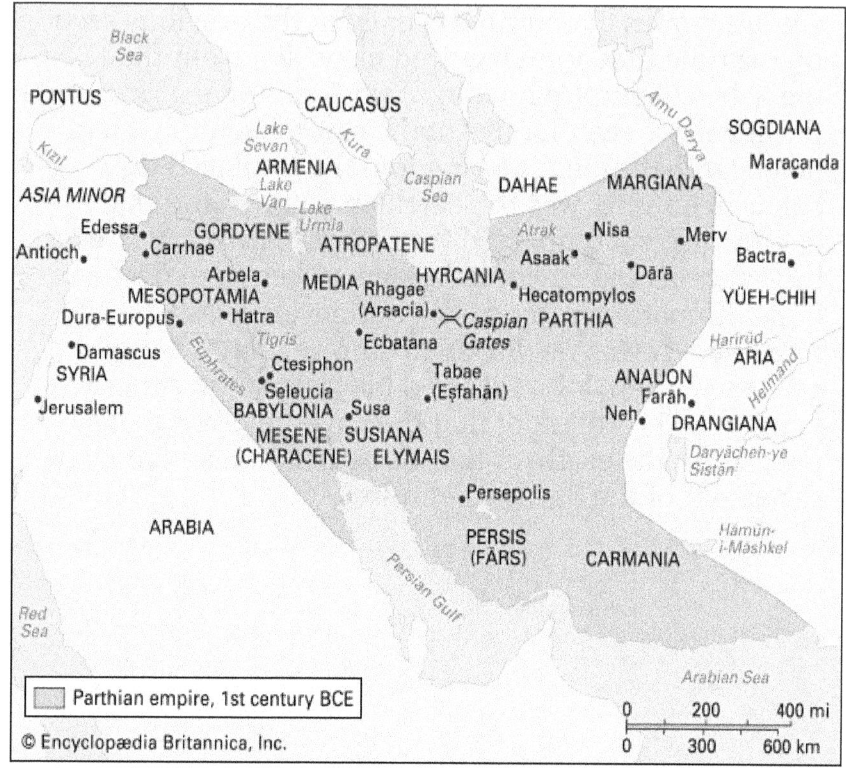

The Parthian empire ceased to exist in the year 224 AD. The empire that replaced it, was the Sasanian empire. This was the last of the seven kingdoms mentioned by the angel, for this was the last kingdom to reign over the city of Babylon. Under the Parthian empire, the city of Babylon had steadily fallen into ruin, and even though it experienced a brief revival under the Sassanid Persians, it never approached its former greatness. In the year 610 AD, the prophet Mohammed, introduced Islam into the earth. Just forty years later, the Sasanian empire ceased to exist, when it fell to Muslim conquest of the land, in the year 650 AD. It was in that conquest, that whatever remained of the city of Babylon, was finally swept away, and in time, was buried beneath the sands.[2] Below is a map showing the extent of the Sasanian empire.

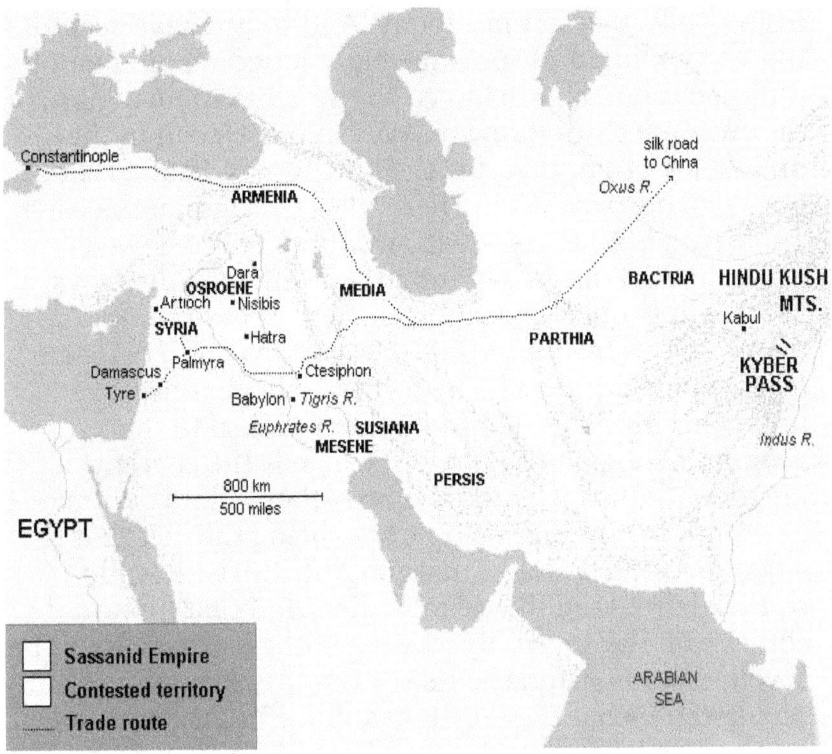

And so, we see that the seven kingdoms referred to by the angel in John's vision, were the seven kingdoms that reigned over the city of Babylon, from its inception, until its demise. So, why did our Lord want us to know about the seven kingdoms, that reigned over the city of Babylon? He revealed this to us, so that we could clearly identify where the Anti-Christ would come from. For the kingdom from where the Anti-Christ will arise, is the kingdom that replaced the last of the seven kingdoms mentioned by the angel, and that is the kingdom of Islam. For Islam, has been in control of that geographic region, from 650 AD, even until today. And so, we have seen that the seven kingdoms, plus the eight kingdom of Islam, that replaced them, all are linked to the geographic region, of the ancient city of Babylon. We have also seen in the previous section, that it is the kingdom of Islam, that our Lord will destroy, when He returns to reign on the earth. That truth is consistent with what the Lord showed Nebuchadnezzar, in his dream. For the scripture says, *"You watched while a stone was cut out without hands, which struck the image on its feet of iron and clay, and broke them in pieces"*. The feet in Nebuchadnezzar's dream, represents the last kingdom linked to the geographic region of Babylon, which is the current kingdom of Islam. There are two other points that need to be mentioned here. The first one, being the fact that the angel revealed to John, that the Anti-Christ would in fact be the eighth king that would arise, and that he would come from the seven. By looking at the link, between the seven kingdoms and the rise of Islam, we can now clearly understand what the angel meant, for in the previous section, we have already seen that the Anti-Christ emerges from the religion of Islam. The second point, is that the final kingdom mentioned in Nebuchadnezzar's dream, refers to the toes of the feet, which were partly of iron and partly of clay. This last kingdom will be made up of a coalition of nations, for the scripture says, *"And in the days of these kings the God of heaven will set up a kingdom"*. Notice that the scripture refers to kings (plural) not king (singular). There were ten toes, on the feet of the last kingdom in Nebuchadnezzar's dream, and as we have seen in the previous section, there are ten kings mentioned by the angel, that will arise from the fourth kingdom, in the last days. Clearly both Nebuchadnezzar's dream, and the angel's explanation of John's vision, are referring to the same kingdoms. And so, we have seen clearly in this section, that the seven kingdoms mentioned by the angel, have all since passed on, and they have been replaced, by the current kingdom, of Islam. Below is a map showing the extent of Islam, in that geographic region, and the world, today.

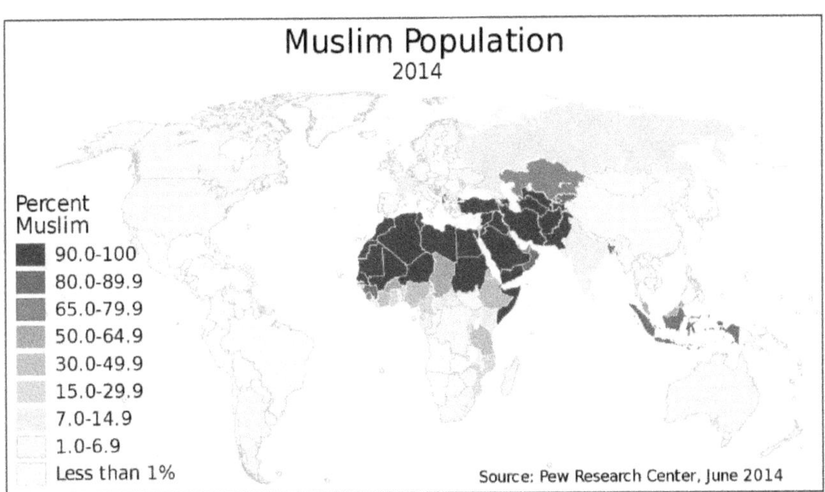

The early signs

Chapter 2

The branch is becoming tender

The nation of Israel

The next key event in chronological sequence, that must take place before our Lord's return, is that natural Israel must once again be restored as a nation, to the land of Israel. Before we look at this key event, I need to explain the difference between natural Israel and spiritual Israel. For there is a natural Israel and there is a spiritual Israel. Natural Israel are all the descendants of Abraham, after the flesh. The new testament refers to them as the circumcision (Ephesians 2:11), or Jews. The world refers to them as Jews, and they refer to themselves, as Israelis or Jews. Spiritual Israel on the other hand, are all those who have believed in the gospel of Jesus Christ, which includes both Jews and gentiles alike (Galatians 6:15-16). Natural Israel falls under the old covenant, while spiritual Israel falls under the new covenant. Within natural Israel, there has always been a remnant, which have also become a part of spiritual Israel. They are the descendants of Abraham after the flesh, who have also believed in the gospel of Jesus Christ. As an example, the apostle Paul, would fall into this category. For now, however, the clear majority of natural Israel do not believe the gospel, and thus still fall under the old covenant. Only those who are part of spiritual Israel however, are saved and go to heaven when they die. For the old covenant was never a covenant of salvation, but rather a covenant of laws pertaining to this life only (for more detail on this subject see my book "The Two Gospels Explained"). So, what purpose does the old covenant serve today? God uses the old covenant, to bring natural Israel to the place where they can believe the gospel, and thus be saved.

> *Galatians 3:24 "Therefore the law was our tutor to bring us to Christ, that we might be justified by faith."*

In the scripture quoted above, the apostle Paul explains that the law, which is the old covenant, is Israel's tutor, leading them to Christ. For our Lord Jesus said, that the law testifies of Him (John 5:39). The old covenant is becoming obsolete, and is ready to vanish away (Hebrews 8:13). But until God has brought all those of the circumcision into His kingdom, it remains in place. For the scripture teaches us, that their covenant remains in place for the present time, until the time of the reformation (Hebrews 9:10). The time of reformation will only take place, when our Lord Jesus returns to the earth. All through the old testament, the Lord spoke through His prophets, telling the children of Israel, that because of their persistent rebellion against Him, they would be removed from the land of Israel, and be scattered throughout the nations of the world. The first time this happened was in the year 604 BC, when the Babylonian empire destroyed Jerusalem and the temple. At that time, the Jews were taken captive to Babylon. Even before that event however, most of Israel had already been dispersed, throughout the nations of the world. In the year 450 BC, the Jews were partially restored to their land, and the temple was rebuilt. But they were never a sovereign nation again, as they always fell under the rule of some foreign power. And even when our Lord Jesus came to the earth to die on the cross, Israel was being ruled by the

The branch is becoming tender

Roman empire. In the year 70 AD, God's prophecies were finally fulfilled. Jerusalem and the temple were destroyed, and the rest of Israel were scattered throughout the world. All through the old testament, when our Lord prophesied to Israel about them being scattered throughout the nations, at the same time the Lord also told them that in the latter times, He would once again, bring them back to the land of Israel, that He gave to their fathers. There are many prophecies in scripture that speak of this event that would take place.

Jeremiah 30:3 "For behold, the days are coming,' says the Lord, 'that I will bring back from captivity My people Israel and Judah,' says the Lord. 'And I will cause them to return to the land that I gave to their fathers, and they shall possess it.'"

The above quoted prophecy, given by the Holy Spirit through the prophet Jeremiah, speaks of Israel and Judah, coming back to the land given to them by God. This prophecy refers to natural Israel, not spiritual Israel. Let me say here, that the Lord has also given us numerous prophecies in scripture, about the gathering of spiritual Israel to the land of Israel, when He returns to reign on the earth. For the church (spiritual Israel) will reign over the earth with our Lord Jesus, when He returns to the earth for His millennial reign. And at that time, we will dwell in the much-enlarged geographic location, of the land of Israel. Therefore, we must not confuse that event, with this one prophesied by Jeremiah, for the two events are not the same. This event, refers only to natural Israel, being returned to the land that God has given to their fathers.

The branch is becoming tender

Jeremiah 16:14-16 "Therefore behold, the days are coming," says the Lord, "that it shall no more be said, 'The Lord lives who brought up the children of Israel from the land of Egypt,' (15) but, 'The Lord lives who brought up the children of Israel from the land of the north and from all the lands where He had driven them.' For I will bring them back into their land which I gave to their fathers. (16) "Behold, I will send for many fishermen," says the Lord, "and they shall fish them; and afterward I will send for many hunters, and they shall hunt them from every mountain and every hill, and out of the holes of the rocks."

At the turn of the last century, more and more Jews, started to return to the land of Israel. As the end of the age draws to a close, God will accelerate their return. In the above passage of scripture, the Lord shows us just how relentless He will be, in bringing the Jews back into their land. For He says that He, "will send for many fishermen, ... and they shall fish them; and afterward I will send for many hunters, and they shall hunt them from every mountain and every hill, and out of the holes of the rocks." And so, although the key event, of gathering natural Israel into the land of Israel has begun, it is nowhere near completion, for there are still more Jews that live outside of Israel, than in Israel. In 1975, there were approximately eleven million Jews living outside of Israel. Today, that number has reduced to eight million. There is coming a time however, when there will be no Jews living outside of Israel. This key event is far advanced, and will be completed in the not too distant future. The Lord has said that He would gather all of Israel into their land. And so, for those Jews who choose

The branch is becoming tender

not to go back to Israel of their own free will, the earth will see a rise in anti-Semitism, once again. God will use this, to drive the Jews back to their land of promise. Because the clear majority of Jews that live outside of Israel today, reside in the United States of America, over the coming years, there will be a gradual growth of anti-Semitism in that nation. In the natural, that may seem impossible now, but nevertheless it will happen. According to new data from the Anti-Defamation League (ADL). In its annual Audit of Anti-Semitic Incidents, Anti-Semitic incidents in the U.S. surged more than one-third in 2016, and have jumped 86 percent in the first quarter of 2017. The ADL reports that there has been a massive increase in the amount of harassment of American Jews, particularly since November of this year, and a doubling in the amount of anti-Semitic bullying and vandalism at non-denominational K-12 grade schools.[3] Anti-Semitism, will continue to rise throughout the world as we draw close to the end of the age, for God will ensure that all Jews are brought back to Israel.

Ezekiel 20:32-38 "What you have in your mind shall never be, when you say, 'We will be like the Gentiles, like the families in other countries, serving wood and stone.' (33) "As I live," says the Lord God, "surely with a mighty hand, with an outstretched arm, and with fury poured out, I will rule over you. (34) I will bring you out from the peoples and gather you out of the countries where you are scattered, with a mighty hand, with an outstretched arm, and with fury poured out. (35) And I will bring you into the wilderness of the peoples, and there I will plead My case with you face to face. (36) Just as I pleaded My case with your

The branch is becoming tender

fathers in the wilderness of the land of Egypt, so I will plead My case with you," says the Lord God. (37) "I will make you pass under the rod, and I will bring you into the bond of the covenant; (38) I will purge the rebels from among you, and those who transgress against Me; I will bring them out of the country where they dwell, but they shall not enter the land of Israel. Then you will know that I am the Lord."

In the above passage of scripture, the Lord gives us further insight, into the event of the gathering of the Jews, to the land of Israel. For He tells us, that even though the Jews have desired to live among the world, and become like the rest of the world, He will not allow that to happen. For they are His, and with a mighty hand, with an outstretched arm, and with fury poured out, He will rule over them once again. God tells us, that He will bring them out of the countries where they are scattered, with a mighty hand, with an outstretched arm, and with fury poured out. In other words, for those Jews who resist returning to Israel, they will experience more than enough persecution, to make them change their minds. I want you to also notice, that it is only after they have returned to Israel as a nation, that God will then plead His case, with that nation. In other words, God's agenda is to first bring them back to Israel, and only once that is accomplished, will He then add them to spiritual Israel. When our Lord tells Israel in the above passage, that He will make them pass under the rod, He is referring to the fact that He will make sure that all have been accounted for, and that none have been left out. For that term, refers to how shepherds in biblical days, would count their flock of sheep, by making them pass under his rod, as he counted them. But

The branch is becoming tender

I also want you to notice, that not all who return to Israel, will be brought into spiritual Israel. For our Lord says, that even though He will bring them out of the countries where they currently dwell, He will still purge the rebels and those who transgress against Him, from among them, and those whom He purges, shall not enter Israel (speaking of spiritual Israel). Something else is revealed to us in this passage, that is of significance, for our Lord says that He will bring Israel into the wilderness, and there He will plead His case with them. When we look at the section that deals with the two witnesses, we will see that it is in fact in the wilderness, that God's prophets will preach the gospel to the children of Israel.

> *Ezekiel 36:24-28 "For I will take you from among the nations, gather you out of all countries, and bring you into your own land. (25) Then I will sprinkle clean water on you, and you shall be clean; I will cleanse you from all your filthiness and from all your idols. (26) I will give you a new heart and put a new spirit within you; I will take the heart of stone out of your flesh and give you a heart of flesh. (27) I will put My Spirit within you and cause you to walk in My statutes, and you will keep My judgments and do them. (28) Then you shall dwell in the land that I gave to your fathers; you shall be My people, and I will be your God."*

The above quoted prophecy, given by the Holy Spirit through the prophet Ezekiel, helps us to more clearly understand God's sequence of events for natural Israel. For notice, that God says that He will first gather Israel from among the nations, and bring them into the land of Israel. And so, we see that even though God is

The branch is becoming tender

bringing them back into their land as a nation, that they will not yet be saved as a nation. God then says, that only after He has brought them back into their land, that He will cleanse them. When our Lord says that He will cleanse Israel, He speaks of cleansing them with clean water. In other words, He will initially cleanse them with the washing of the water by His word (Ephesians 5:26). Currently, most Israelis, are not adherents to the law of Moses. But we have already seen, that it is the law that is Israel's tutor, that will bring them to Christ. And so, there is coming a time when Israel as a nation, will once again embrace the law of Moses, and walk in that law. Obviously, that time has not yet come. When that time comes however, God says that He will give them a new heart, and put His Spirit into their hearts. It is only those who are born-again, that receive a new heart, and the Spirit of God takes up residence in their hearts. And so, it is at that time, that Israel as a nation, will be saved, and thus they will become part of spiritual Israel. But their time has not yet come.

Isaiah 66:8 "Who has heard such a thing? Who has seen such things? Shall the earth be made to give birth in one day? Or shall a nation be born at once? For as soon as Zion was in labor, she gave birth to her children."

At the turn of the twentieth century, God began to bring His prophecies to pass, as more and more Jews began to return to the land of Israel. In the year 1948, the prophecy given by Isaiah quoted above, came to pass. For in one day, the nation of natural Israel was once again established in the land of Israel. The first time that Israel was restored to their land of promise in 450 BC, we saw that they rebuilt the temple, but they were not restored as a sovereign nation. This time we see that Israel have been restored as a sovereign nation, but they have not yet rebuilt their temple.

Romans 11:25-26 "For I do not desire, brethren, that you should be ignorant of this mystery, lest you should be wise in your own opinion, that blindness in part has happened to Israel until the fullness of the Gentiles has come in. (26) And so, all Israel will be saved, as it is written: "The Deliverer will come out of Zion, and He will turn away ungodliness from Jacob."

Natural Israel are not yet in that place where they, as a nation, can come into the kingdom of God. But, as revealed to us by the Holy Spirit in the book of Romans quoted above, there is coming a time when all the gentiles who have been chosen by God, will have come into the kingdom. Before that time, all of natural Israel will have been brought into the land of Israel. And so, when the fullness of the gentiles have come into the kingdom, the blindness that has happened to Israel will be removed, and thus natural Israel will believe the gospel and be saved. However, as we draw closer to the end of the age, there will be an increase in the number of Jewish believers. But their numbers will still be small, in relation to the full population of Israel. The reason for that is because their time has not yet come. But nevertheless, there is coming a time when there will no longer be Jews, living outside of Israel.

Israel's territory will increase

The branch is becoming tender

Numbers 34:1-12 "Then the Lord spoke to Moses, saying, (2) "Command the children of Israel, and say to them: 'When you come into the land of Canaan, this is the land that shall fall to you as an inheritance--the land of Canaan to its boundaries. (3) Your southern border shall be from the Wilderness of Zin along the border of Edom; then your southern border shall extend eastward to the end of the Salt Sea; (4) your border shall turn from the southern side of the Ascent of Akrabbim, continue to Zin, and be on the south of Kadesh Barnea; then it shall go on to Hazar Addar, and continue to Azmon; (5) the border shall turn from Azmon to the Brook of Egypt, and it shall end at the Sea. (6) 'As for the western border, you shall have the Great Sea for a border; this shall be your western border. (7) 'And this shall be your northern border: From the Great Sea you shall mark out your border line to Mount Hor; (8) from Mount Hor you shall mark out your border to the entrance of Hamath; then the direction of the border shall be toward Zedad; (9) the border shall proceed to Ziphron, and it shall end at Hazar Enan. This shall be your northern border. (10) 'You shall mark out your eastern border from Hazar Enan to Shepham; (11) the border shall go down from Shepham to Riblah on the east side of Ain; the border shall go down and reach to the eastern side of the Sea of Chinnereth; (12) the border shall go down along the Jordan, and it shall end at the Salt Sea. This shall be your land with its surrounding boundaries.'"

The above passage of scripture reveals to us the geographic borders of the state of Israel, that God had

The branch is becoming tender

given to them, through the prophet Moses. Under the reign of king David, Israel reached the boundaries given to them, by God. On today's map, those borders included current day Israel (including the territories that the world claims, Israel occupies illegally), half of current day Lebanon, and the south-western part of current day Syria. After king David's reign however, Israel consistently rebelled against God, and her borders were slowly reduced in size, until they finally went into captivity in Babylon, and ceased to exist as a sovereign nation. While Israel was in exile in Babylon, the Lord gave the prophet Ezekiel, a vision of the geographic borders of the state of Israel, that would exist in the last days. That vision is recorded in the following passage of scripture. Many have thought, that Ezekiel's vision (Ezekiel, chapters 40 to 47), refers to the period of our Lord's millennial reign on the earth. However, the only part of Ezekiel's vision, that refers to the period of our Lord's millennial reign, is the passage where our Lord showed the prophet, the river of life that will proceed from the temple, during His millennial reign (Ezekiel 47:1-12). The rest of Ezekiel's vision, refers to the state of Israel, the temple, and the priesthood, that will exist, in the last days.

Ezekiel 47:13-21 "Thus says the Lord God: "These are the borders by which you shall divide the land as an inheritance among the twelve tribes of Israel. Joseph shall have two portions. (14) You shall inherit it equally with one another; for I raised My hand in an oath to give it to your fathers, and this land shall fall to you as your inheritance. (15) "This shall be the border of the land on the north: from the Great Sea, by the road to Hethlon, as one goes to Zedad, (16) Hamath, Berothah, Sibraim (which is between the border of Damascus and the border of Hamath), to Hazar Hatticon (which is on the border of Hauran). (17) Thus, the boundary shall be from the Sea to Hazar Enan, the border of Damascus; and as for the north, northward, it is the border of Hamath. This is the north side. (18) "On the east side you shall mark out the border from between Hauran and Damascus, and between Gilead and the land of Israel, along the Jordan, and along the eastern side of the sea. This is the east side. (19) "The south side, toward the South, shall be from Tamar to the waters of Meribah by Kadesh, along the brook to the Great Sea. This is the south side, toward the South. (20) "The west side shall be the Great Sea, from the southern boundary until one comes to a point opposite Hamath. This is the west side. (21) "Thus, you shall divide this land among yourselves according to the tribes of Israel."

The branch is becoming tender

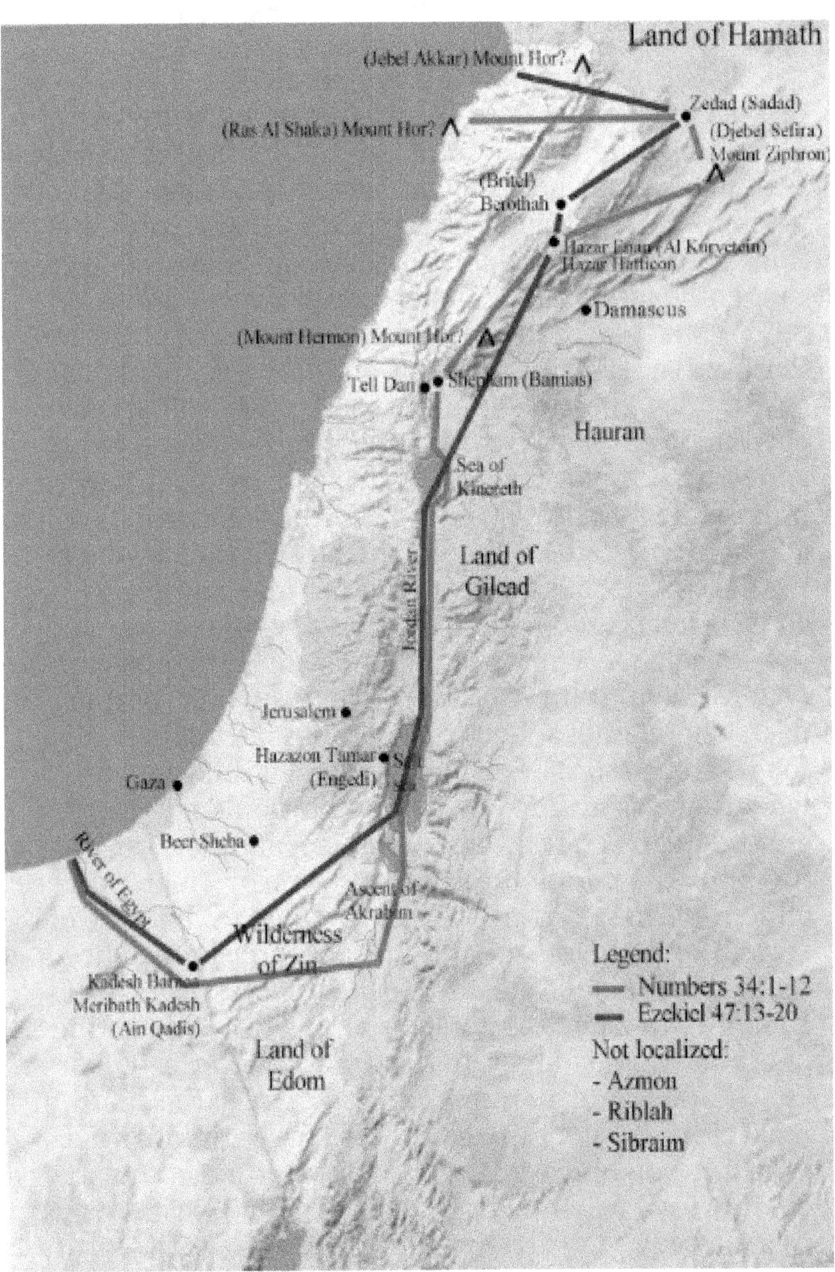

The branch is becoming tender

As can be seen, when compared on the above map, the vision given to Ezekiel, and the territory given to Moses as quoted earlier, are almost identical. And so, we see that God has not deviated from the original territory given to the children of Israel, in that He has prophesied that Israel will once again possess that self-same territory. Currently, modern day Israel occupies most of the territory as recorded in Ezekiel's vision, except for the Palestinian territories of Gaza and the West Bank, half of current day Lebanon, and the south-western part of current day Syria. Those four territories are still to be added to the state of Israel, as it exists today. It may seem impossible now, but nevertheless, those territories will be added to the state of Israel, for God said they would be. In the past, Israel has added to her territory, through wars she has fought. For example, the 1967 six-day war added the so-called, occupied territories, which included the city of Jerusalem. It must be mentioned however, that in the past, when Israel added to her territory through wars fought, those wars were always wars of self-defence, i.e. when she was invaded by those who would try to annihilate the state of Israel. And so, another war will be fought in the middle east, the outcome of which, will see all four of those territories, being added to the state of Israel. Nevertheless, this will be a war of self-defence for the state of Israel. It is interesting to note, that Israel's Defence Minister, has gone on record to say that, "the next war will be fought on two fronts, with Hezbollah along Israel's northern border and Gaza in the south, regardless of where the initial conflict begins or what causes it", and he went on to warn, that Israel's next conflict with Lebanon, would also involve Syria.[4] As we have already seen, it is precisely these territories, that God still has to restore to the nation of Israel. And so, when the conflict finally erupts, God will work a miracle, and deliver to Israel, the four territories mentioned, for all Muslims living in those territories, will evacuate those territories, as a result of the conflict. We have seen in this section, that Israel is anticipating that it will eventually go to war with Hezbollah, which is based in Lebanon, Syria and Gaza. What is interesting to note about Hezbollah, is that it is a Shi'a Islamist political party and militant group. So why is that important? There are two main streams in the Muslim faith, i.e. Sunni and Shi'a. Currently, there is a power struggle taking place between the two leading states of both religious streams, i.e. Saudi Arabia (of the Sunni stream) and Iran (of the Shi'a stream). Because the war with Israel, will be with the Shi'a supported Hezbollah, the rest of the Arab world will not interfere, as they will want to see Iran's influence in the middle east, curbed. One of the profound outcomes, that will occur as a result of this war, is that not only will God restore Israel, to the full borders He has promised her, but this conflict will also result in the destruction of the Dome of the Rock, and the Al-Aksa Mosque, on the temple mount. This will obviously pave the way for the nation of Israel, to once again build the Lord's temple on that site, and that construction will go ahead. The world's political landscape would have changed sufficiently by that time, so that none will interfere with either the change to Israel's borders, or the building of the temple. The Lord revealed to us through Ezekiel's vision, that it will be at that time, that Israel will divide her territory by lot, to the twelve tribes of Israel. And so, we see that this event will also only take place, once all of Israel have returned to that nation, so that her territory can be divided to all her tribes. The nation of Israel, in their current spiritual condition, would never allow their land to be divided by lot. And so, God will work a miracle in that nation, to return them to observing the law of Moses. Currently, Israel has no idea which tribe each Jew is descended from, and so it would be impossible for them to divide their territory by lot. Nevertheless, God will intervene between now and that time, so that when the time comes, Israel will be well able to divide her territory by lot. It may be, that DNA testing will be used, to determine who belongs to which tribe. Or it may even be, that the Lord will revive the use of the Urim, by the priests, to determine who belongs to which tribe. Just as He did, when Israel returned from captivity in Babylon, and the priests had to consult the Urim, to determine which were Levites, and which weren't (Nehemiah 7:65). But I need to emphasize, that even though Israel will once again walk in the old covenant, she will still not at that time be saved, as it is only those who partake of the new covenant, that are saved.

Luke 21:24 "And they will fall by the edge of the sword, and be led away captive into all nations. And Jerusalem will be trampled by Gentiles until the times of the Gentiles are fulfilled."

Our Lord Jesus, taught us in the above passage of scripture, that from the time of the destruction of the second temple (which took place in 70 AD), that Jerusalem would be trampled by the gentiles, until the times of the gentiles are fulfilled. And that is exactly what has happened. For in the year 70 AD, the population of the city of Jerusalem was one hundred percent Jewish. However, after its destruction in that same year, the Jewish population dropped to zero. Since that time, the city of Jerusalem has been populated primarily, by

The branch is becoming tender

gentiles. However, over the centuries, the Jewish population in the city has slowly increased, and presently, Jews account for approximately sixty percent of Jerusalem's population. Nevertheless, a large part of Jerusalem is still occupied by gentiles. And so, even though we are seeing a diminished trampling of the city of Jerusalem by the gentiles, the times of the gentiles have not yet been fulfilled. It is only when Israel increases her territory, as discussed in this section, that we will also see the city of Jerusalem being fully restored to Israel, once again.

The temple rebuilt

We have seen in the previous section, that God will work the miracle of restoring Israel to the full territory, that He originally gave to them through the prophet Moses. And we have also seen, that at the same time, that God will restore the city of Jerusalem, to the full control of the Jews. As we will see in this section, the temple will be rebuilt in the city of Jerusalem. But we need to understand, that when this event takes place in the state of Israel, that it will not be a small fringe group of Orthodox Jews, that will bring this about, while the rest of the nation continues with their secular lifestyles. As I have already mentioned, God will work a miracle in that nation, that will cause the whole nation, to return to observing the laws of Moses. And so, the whole nation, will be involved in the rebuilding of the temple in the city of Jerusalem.

Hosea 3:4-5 "For the children of Israel shall abide many days without king or prince, without sacrifice or sacred pillar, without ephod or teraphim. (5) Afterward the children of Israel shall return and

The branch is becoming tender

seek the Lord their God and David their king. They shall fear the Lord and His goodness in the latter days."

In the above passage of scripture, the Lord tells Israel that they would abide many days without a leader, and without the temple. Since that prophecy, Israel has never had both a leader and the temple, restored at the same time. She had the temple restored, in approximately 450 BC, but as we have said, she was a not a sovereign nation at that time, and so she had no leader restored to her. The second temple was destroyed in 70 AD. Since that time, her sovereignty as a nation has been restored in 1948, and she now has leaders, but no temple. But God stated, that in the latter days, the Jews would return to Israel, and seek the Lord their God, and fear the Lord, and His goodness. In other words, the nation of Israel, once they returned to Israel, would once again, turn to God, as a nation. And the Lord clearly implied in this passage, that He would restore to them, both their leaders and the temple. Modern Israel today, is mainly secular, and as such, she is very far from seeking the fear of the Lord, as a nation. When we read the prophetic vision of Ezekiel (chapters 40 to 47), we see an Israel, that is fully observant of the laws of Moses. And so, we see that God will work a miracle in that nation, to return that nation to following the laws of Moses. As we have already seen, it is only after the territories, spoken about in the previous section, have been added to Israel, that she will then build the temple once again. For in the following passage of scripture, our Lord instructs Israel to make provision for the temple area, when they divide their land by lot. Clearly, the temple will not be built prior to Israel dividing their land by lot. The event of those territories being added to Israel, will be the catalyst that God will use, to restore Israel to observing the law of Moses, as a nation once again. For through Ezekiel's vision, the Lord revealed to us all the ordinances that Israel will implement, and follow, during that period (Ezekiel chapters 40 to 47).

Ezekiel 45:1-3 "Moreover, when you divide the land by lot into inheritance, you shall set apart a district for the Lord, a holy section of the land; its length shall be twenty-five thousand cubits, and the width ten thousand. It shall be holy throughout its territory all around. (2) Of this there shall be a square plot for the sanctuary, five hundred by five hundred rods, with fifty cubits around it for an open space. (3) So, this is the district you shall measure: twenty-five thousand cubits long and ten thousand wide; in it shall be the sanctuary, the Most Holy Place."

And so, the next key event that must take place chronologically, before our Lord Jesus returns, is that the third Jewish temple must be built in the city of Jerusalem. When our Lord Jesus ministered on the earth, He prophesied in Luke's gospel, that the second Jewish temple in which He was standing at the time, would be destroyed (Luke 21:6). That prophecy was fulfilled in the year 70 AD, when that temple was destroyed by the Roman army. Our Lord then went on to prophecy, about another temple that would be built.

Mark 13:14 "So when you see the 'Abomination of desolation,' spoken of by Daniel the prophet, standing where it ought not" (let the reader understand), "then let those who are in Judea flee to the mountains."

In Mark's gospel quoted above, when our Lord referred to "the abomination of desolation", standing where he ought not to stand, He was referring to the Anti-Christ standing in the temple of God. For that is the abomination of desolation that the prophet Daniel spoke about in the vision that he saw (Daniel 12:11). In fact, Daniel was shown two abominations of desolation. The first one that he saw, occurred in the year 163 BC (Daniel 11:31). It was as a result of that event, that the Jewish Feast of Dedication was introduced to the Jewish calendar (John 10:22). The Feast of Dedication is a celebration of the cleansing of the second temple after the Jews defeated Antiochus Epiphanes, a Syrian King who invaded Jerusalem, defiled the temple by placing an image of Zeus in the temple, and offering a pig on the altar[5]. The second abomination of desolation that Daniel saw, was the Anti-Christ standing in the temple, at the end of the age. It is this second vision given to Daniel, to which our Lord Jesus was referring, when He prophesied. The reason why Mark interjects in this passage of scripture, the comment, "let the reader understand", is because some have thought that our Lord was referring to the destruction of the second temple that took place in 70 AD, as the abomination of desolation. But that is not the case at all, and in fact Matthew's account also records the words, "whoever reads, let him understand", when recounting our Lord's referral to the abomination of desolation (Matthew 24:15). For in both Mark and Matthew's accounts, our Lord was referring to the Anti-Christ standing in the temple of God, at the end of the age. As we will see later in this teaching, it was in Luke's gospel account of our Lord's teaching on end time events, that our Lord referred to the destruction of the second temple (Luke 21:20). Which is why the Holy Spirit did not impress upon Luke to add the comment, "whoever reads, let him understand", as He did with Mark and Matthew. And so, we see that Jesus clearly taught us that the third Jewish temple would be in place, by the time that the Anti-Christ is revealed in the earth.

2 Thessalonians 2:3-4 "Let no one deceive you by any means; for that Day will not come unless the falling away comes first, and the man of sin is revealed, the son of perdition, (4) who opposes and exalts himself above all that is called God or that is worshiped, so that he sits as God in the temple of God, showing himself that he is God."

In the above quoted passage of scripture, the apostle Paul in writing to the church in Thessalonica, by the inspiration of the Holy Spirit, teaches us that the son of perdition, who is also called the Anti-Christ, will one day sit in the temple of God. The Anti-Christ will do this, to show himself to the world, that he is god. Therefore, we can clearly see that God's temple will be in place, before the end of the age. When Paul wrote his letter to the church in Thessalonica, the second Jewish temple had not yet been destroyed, and so those disciples knew exactly which temple, Paul was referring to in his letter.

Revelation 11:1-2 "Then I was given a reed like a measuring rod. And the angel stood, saying, "Rise and measure the temple of God, the altar, and those who worship there. (2) But leave out the court which is outside the temple, and do not measure it,

The branch is becoming tender

*for it has been given to the Gentiles. And they will
tread the holy city underfoot for forty-two months."*

In the book of Revelation quoted above, our Lord
Jesus gave the apostle John, a vision of the temple that
would be in existence before the Lord returns to the earth.
At the time that John received his vision from the Lord,
the second temple had already been destroyed, in
fulfilment of our Lord's prophecy (Mark 13:2). For John
received his vision from the Lord Jesus, approximately
twenty years after the second temple had already been
destroyed. And so, the temple in John's vision, referred to
the third Jewish temple, still to be built. We know that it
was a physical temple that John saw in his vision, for he
was given a measuring rod to measure its structure. The
last part of the passage quoted, states that the gentiles will
tread the holy city underfoot for forty-two months. This is
referring to the period when the Anti-Christ will reign
from the temple, for he has been allowed to rule for forty-
two months (Revelation 13:5).

*Ezekiel 43:10-11 "Son of man, describe the
temple to the house of Israel, that they may be
ashamed of their iniquities; and let them measure
the pattern. (11) And if they are ashamed of all that
they have done, make known to them the design of
the temple and its arrangement, its exits and its
entrances, its entire design and all its ordinances, all
its forms and all its laws. Write it down in their
sight, so that they may keep its whole design and all
its ordinances, and perform them."*

In the above quoted passage of scripture, the Lord
gave the prophet Ezekiel, a detailed vision of the layout of

the third Jewish temple, and its operation, when that temple is eventually built. That account can be read in Ezekiel, chapters forty to forty-six. Currently in the natural, it seems impossible that Israel would ever be able to build the third temple. This is mainly because of the conflict that would erupt in the middle east, between the Muslim nations and modern-day Israel, because the Muslim nations hold the site of the "temple mount", as one of their most holy sites. As we have already seen however, God will bring about the changes required, for Israel to be able to go ahead and finally rebuild the third temple. We are already seeing the complete disruptions in the Muslim nations surrounding Israel (it has been called the Arab spring, among other terms) and God has only just begun. When it is all over, circumstances would have changed in the middle east, to the point that Israel will be able to build God's temple. Obviously once the temple is built, Israel will once again practice temple worship, as taught under the old covenant. This will occur, because more and more Jews, will return to walking in the laws of the old covenant. In this respect, it is interesting to note, that currently, the orthodox Jews (who strictly adhere to the laws of the old covenant) are the fastest growing segment of the Jewish population, in the world today[6].

Ezekiel 43:12 "This is the law of the temple: The whole area surrounding the mountaintop is most holy. Behold, this is the law of the temple."

In reference to the site, which today is called "the temple mount", God, in the above passage of scripture, has stated that, "the whole area surrounding the mountaintop is most holy". Currently, the Muslim shrines called the Dome of the Rock, and the Al-Aksa Mosque, are placed on that site. God will not allow His temple to be built, alongside any other shrine. And so, there is coming a day, when those Muslim shrines will be removed. This will take place, when the time of the gentiles has been fulfilled, and the city of Jerusalem is once again restored, to the Jewish people (Luke 21:24).

The fullness of the Gentiles

Matthew 24:14 "And this gospel of the kingdom will be preached in all the world as a witness to all the nations, and then the end will come."

Another key event that must take place before our Lord Jesus returns to the earth, is that the fullness of the gentiles must be brought into the church (Romans 11:25). As quoted above in Matthew's gospel, our Lord Jesus said that the gospel of the kingdom would be preached in all the world, as a witness to all the nations, and then the end would come. The word of the Lord Jesus will be fulfilled. Every nation on the earth, would have heard the gospel preached, before He returns. But I want you to notice that our Lord did not say, that the gospel would be preached in all the world, *at the same time.* He also did not say, that the gospel would be preached to all nations, *all the time until the end.* From the start of the church age until now, at some point in time, most if not all nations, have had the gospel preached in them, as a witness to that nation. However, when they heard it preached, not all nations responded positively to the message of the gospel. You will recall that our Lord Jesus taught us, that there will be cities that will not be receptive to the message of the gospel. In those instances, those sent to preach to those cities, were to leave those cities and wipe off the dust from their feet, as a testimony against them.

> *Luke 10:10-11 "But whatever city you enter, and they do not receive you, go out into its streets and say, (11) 'The very dust of your city which clings to us we wipe off against you. Nevertheless, know this, that the kingdom of God has come near you."*

That same principle is applicable to nations as well. In other words, just as certain cities will not be receptive to the message of the gospel, so there will be certain nations, that will not be receptive to the message of the gospel. Nevertheless, those nations will have no excuse on that day, for the kingdom of God has come near to them, but they refused to hear the message preached. An example of a nation today, that is not receptive to the message of the gospel, would be Saudi Arabia. If you study church history, you will find that over the centuries, there have also been many nations that have responded positively to the message of the gospel preached. Those nations have seen great revivals in their midst, and during those times of revival, multitudes were added to the kingdom of God. However, many of those same nations, have since become hardened to the gospel, and there is no longer any significant move of God in their midst. Many of those nations have received their last call, and will not receive another. Wales is an example of just such a nation. At the start of the twentieth century, there was a great revival that swept over that nation, and multitudes were added to the kingdom of God. Many from around the world went to that nation, to experience what God was doing there. But instead of building on that foundation, those saints let the work of God die, and there is no longer

The branch is becoming tender

any significant move of God in Wales today. There are very few nations in the earth today, if any, that have not had the gospel preached in them, at some point in their history. We are entering a time, when some nations are about to receive their last call. Some nations will respond, and experience a mighty move of God in their midst, and the Lord will add many to His kingdom, but there are also some that will refuse to hear the gospel message, and will thus experience their appropriate judgement, on that day. The nation of South Africa, in which I reside, is receiving her last call at this present time, and even though in the natural, it seems as if she is not responding to her call, the Lord has spoken clear prophetic words over this nation, that He will bring in one last harvest, from this nation. The nation of the United States, received her last call towards the end of the last century, and it seems as if she has not responded to that call, for that nation is experiencing a decline in her spirituality. But nevertheless, there is coming a time, when the last call to all the gentile nations, will be made in the earth, and then the fullness of the gentiles would have been brought into the kingdom. In other words, there is coming a day when no more gentiles will be saved, because the fullness of their number would have come into the kingdom of God.

Acts 15:14-18 "Simon has declared how God at the first visited the Gentiles to take out of them a people for His name. (15) And with this the words of the prophets agree, just as it is written: (16) 'After this I will return and will rebuild the tabernacle of david, which has fallen down; I will rebuild its ruins, and I will set it up; (17) so that the rest of mankind may seek the Lord, even all the gentiles who are called by My name, says the Lord who does all these

The branch is becoming tender

things.' (18) "Known to God from eternity are all His works."

    In the passage of scripture quoted above from the book of Acts, the Holy Spirit through the apostle James, tells us that there is a finite number of gentiles that are to be saved. For He says, *"even all the Gentiles who are called by My name"*. When the Holy Spirit says, "all the Gentiles", He is confirming that none that are called by His name, will be left out. But He is also saying that there will be none added, after all have been taken in. You will recall that our Lord stated that the time will come when He will shut the door, and none will be allowed into the kingdom, after that door is shut (Luke 13:25).

    Romans 11:25 "For I do not desire, brethren, that you should be ignorant of this mystery, lest you should be wise in your own opinion, that blindness in part has happened to Israel until the fullness of the Gentiles has come in."

    In the apostle Paul's letter to the church at Rome quoted above, the Holy Spirit clearly tells us that there is coming a time, when the fullness of the gentiles would have come into the kingdom. Again, the Holy Spirit clearly tells us that there is a finite number of gentiles that will be saved. For He says that, "the fullness of the Gentiles will come in". Notice that with regards to the timeline of the key events that must take place before our Lord returns, that the event of the fullness of the gentiles coming into the kingdom, must take place before natural Israel can be added to the kingdom. If we look back at the history of the church, we can more clearly understand how God will bring to pass, that which He has stated in this passage of

The branch is becoming tender

scripture. When the church began, she was one hundred percent Jewish, and there were no gentile believers. Over the years, more and more gentile believers were added, and fewer Jewish believers were added, until the church became predominately gentile, with a very small remnant of Jewish believers. Until very recent times, that has remained the status quo in the church. In 1948 when Israel once again became a sovereign nation, there were a total of twenty-five Jewish believers in that nation[7]. Since that time, the number of Jewish believers has steadily increased over the years. And today, there are over two hundred small Jewish believer fellowships in the nation of Israel. And so, as we draw closer to the end of the age, the number of gentile believers will begin to decline, and the number of Jewish believers will begin to increase. However, although the number of Jewish believers will continue to gradually increase, their numbers relative to the size of the Israeli population, will still remain very small, because Israel will only be brought into the kingdom as a nation, at the end of the age. But with regards to the gentile believers, their decline in numbers will accelerate, as we draw closer to the end of the age. It is no secret, that many nations that at one time had a large Christian population, have over the past few decades, experienced a vast decline in their numbers, relative to the size of the populations of those nations.

Luke 21:24 "And they will fall by the edge of the sword, and be led away captive into all nations. And Jerusalem will be trampled by Gentiles until the times of the Gentiles are fulfilled."

The above passage of scripture records a prophetic statement made by our Lord Jesus. In this passage, our

The branch is becoming tender

Lord was referring to the destruction of Jerusalem, which took place in the year 70 AD. When our Lord made His statement, the population of the city of Jerusalem, was one hundred percent Jewish. After the Jews were removed from Jerusalem in the year 70 AD, for centuries, gentiles accounted for one hundred percent of Jerusalem's population, i.e. no Jews lived there. Jesus stated that the city of Jerusalem would be trampled by gentiles, until the times of the gentiles were fulfilled. When our Lord referred to the times of the gentiles being fulfilled, He was referring to that which the Holy Spirit spoke of, through the apostle Paul in the book of Romans, i.e. the fullness of the gentiles coming into the kingdom of God (Romans 11:25). In other words, our Lord was saying that when the fullness of the gentiles have come into the kingdom, then the city of Jerusalem will once again, be fully restored to the nation of Israel. Over the centuries, the Jewish population of Jerusalem has grown from zero percent, to its current population, of sixty percent. And so, although today we see a diminished trampling of Jerusalem by the gentiles, that number has not yet dropped to zero, and therefore, the fullness of the gentiles are still to come into the kingdom. But as we have already seen, the event that will see Jerusalem no longer being trampled underfoot by gentiles, will take place almost overnight. When that event happens, there will be no more salvations taking place, among the nations of the world. One of the fivefold ministry gifts in the church, is the ministry gift of the evangelist. The primary role of the evangelist, is to add lost souls to the kingdom of God. It is significant, that the two most anointed evangelists in the earth today, i.e. Billy Graham and Reinhard Bonnke, who between them, have been used of the Lord to add millions to the kingdom, have both recently retired from ministry. And there is no indication, that our Lord has raised up evangelists of their stature in the church, to replace them. The reason for that may just be, because the time of the gentiles, is rapidly drawing to a close.

The falling away

Just as the time of the gentiles, is rapidly drawing to a close, so the time of the falling away, is rapidly approaching. This will be a dangerous time for church, for it is during this time, that many believers will lose their salvation, for that is what the term, "falling away", means. Now, more than ever, Christians need to be grounded in the truth of God's word. God's word is always balanced. For example, in Romans chapter eleven, the scripture tells us to consider both the goodness and the severity of God (Romans 11:22). If only the goodness of God is emphasized, then people become deceived into thinking that there is no judgement with God, no matter how badly they behave. On the other hand, if only the severity of God is emphasized, then people become just as deceived into thinking that God is a God of wrath, punishing every wrong move that they make. Both the goodness of God, and the severity of God, are truths that are revealed to us in the bible. But in the natural, they seem to be opposing truths, for how can a good God, at the same time, be severe? That is where the ministry gifts come in, for it is the role of the ministry gifts, to teach the church how to rightly divide the word of truth, i.e. understand God's word.

Ephesians 4:11-14 "And He Himself gave some to be apostles, some prophets, some evangelists, and some pastors and teachers, (12) for the equipping of

The branch is becoming tender

*the saints for the work of ministry, for the edifying of
the body of Christ, (13) till we all come to the unity
of the faith and of the knowledge of the Son of God,
to a perfect man, to the measure of the stature of the
fullness of Christ; (14) that we should no longer be
children, tossed to and fro and carried about with
every wind of doctrine, by the trickery of men, in the
cunning craftiness of deceitful plotting."*

As quoted above, in His letter to the church in
Ephesus, the Holy Spirit tells us that He has placed the
ministry gifts in the church, to bring the Lord's church to
maturity. God expects the ministry gifts to study His
word, so that they can learn to rightly divide the word of
truth (2 Timothy 2:15). For the ministry gifts are stewards
of the mysteries of God (1 Corinthians 4:1). The ministry
gifts are then required, to teach that word of truth, to the
church, declaring God's full counsel. In this manner, the
church can then understand how seemingly contradicting
truths in God's word, in fact support each other. You can
therefore readily see, that any ministry gift that refuses to
teach the full counsel of God, and only emphasises one
aspect of truth, would be instrumental in making the
saints vulnerable, to becoming deceived. It is safe to say
that any ministry, that refuses to declare the full counsel
of God, should be avoided. The apostle Paul, in his last
message to the elders of the church at Ephesus, told them
that he was innocent of the blood of all men, because he
had not neglected to declare the full counsel of God to
them (Acts 20:26-27). Among carnal believers, the full
counsel of God, is not a popular message. Towards the
end of his ministry, the apostle Paul was no longer
welcome in the churches in Asia, including the church at
Ephesus (2 Timothy 1:15). The reason being, that they

could no longer endure sound doctrine, but according to their own desires, because they had itching ears, they found teachers that catered to their carnal desires; and they turned their ears away from the truth, and were turned aside to listen to a false gospel. The apostle John experienced the same thing, in that he and his ministry team, were eventually also not welcomed in certain churches (3 John 1:10).

1 John 2:26-27 "These things I have written to you concerning those who try to deceive you. (27) But the anointing which you have received from Him abides in you, and you do not need that anyone teach you; but as the same anointing teaches you concerning all things, and is true, and is not a lie, and just as it has taught you, you will abide in Him."

But I want you to notice in the above passage of scripture, something that the apostle John teaches us, regarding the anointing of the Holy Spirit. He teaches us that each believer, has the anointing on the inside of them. And it is the anointing of the Holy Spirit within us, which can keep us from being deceived. I have seen whole churches being led astray, out of loyalty to pastors, who have gone after the teachings of false prophets. But I have also seen, even baby Christians, leaving those same churches, because the Holy Spirit had witnessed on the inside of them, that those doctrines were not of God.

Luke 8:13 "But the ones on the rock are those who, when they hear, receive the word with joy; and these have no root, who believe for a while and in time of temptation fall away."

The branch is becoming tender

Since the church began, there have always been those who have fallen away, from following the Lord Jesus. Our Lord Jesus taught us this truth, in the parable of the sower, quoted above. These are people who hear the gospel of salvation, and believe in the Lord Jesus, and are born-again. But, from the time that they are saved, they never grow spiritually. And so, through temptations, they are slowly drawn back into the world. They eventually become so entangled in the things of the world, that they are once again overcome by the world, and stop following the Lord altogether. And thus, they fall away. It is not always baby Christians, that fall away however.

Hebrews 6:4-6 "For it is impossible for those who were once enlightened, and have tasted the heavenly gift, and have become partakers of the Holy Spirit, (5) and have tasted the good word of God and the powers of the age to come, (6) if they fall away, to renew them again to repentance, since they crucify again for themselves the Son of God, and put Him to an open shame."

The Holy Spirit, in the letter to the Hebrew church quoted above, expanded on the truth that even mature believers, can fall away. In this passage of scripture, He speaks about mature believers, who have been filled with the Holy Spirit, and have even operated in the gifts of the Spirit, falling away. Sin cannot be taken lightly. For if sin is left unchecked, it will spread like cancer. In scripture, the Holy Spirit has warned, on more than one occasion, that a little leaven leavens' the whole lump (1 Corinthians 5:6). The apostle Paul stated that he kept his body under, and brought it into subjection, lest after having preached to others, he would himself, be found a castaway (1

The branch is becoming tender

Corinthians 9:27). The Holy Spirit, in the passage of scripture quoted above, clearly teaches us that to fall away, means to lose one's salvation, for He tells us that, "it is impossible... to renew them again to repentance".

2 Thessalonians 2:1-3 "Now, brethren, concerning the coming of our Lord Jesus Christ and our gathering together to Him, we ask you, (2) not to be soon shaken in mind or troubled, either by spirit or by word or by letter, as if from us, as though the day of Christ had come. (3) Let no one deceive you by any means; for that Day, will not come unless the falling away comes first, and the man of sin is revealed, the son of perdition."

In his letter to the church in Thessalonica, the apostle Paul refers to an event called, "the falling away". The falling away that Paul refers to, is an event that will affect the whole church, in the last days. It is during this time, that a significant number of believers, will fall away from following the Lord Jesus. Notice also, that the Holy Spirit says that the falling away, must come first. And so, we see that one of the early key events, that must take place before our Lord's return, is that there must be a falling away that takes place in the church.

1 Timothy 4:1 "Now the Spirit expressly says that in latter times some will depart from the faith, giving heed to deceiving spirits and doctrines of demons."

When the scripture, in first Timothy quoted above, says that some will depart from the faith, it is referring to those who believe in Jesus, and are part of His kingdom.

The branch is becoming tender

It is these believers, that will depart from the faith. Those who fall away from following Christ will not be imposters, pretending to be Christians. For one cannot depart from, or fall away from, that which they were never part of, in the first place. So, what will be the cause of this event called, the falling away? The main cause, will be an increase in false teachings and false doctrines, that will be brought into the church. For the Holy Spirit clearly tells us, that those who give heed to deceiving spirits and doctrines of demons, will be the ones who will depart from the faith, in the last days.

2 Timothy 4:3-4 "For the time will come when they will not endure sound doctrine, but according to their own desires, because they have itching ears, they will heap up for themselves teachers; (4) and they will turn their ears away from the truth, and be turned aside to fables."

In the above passage of scripture, the Holy Spirit gives us further insight into the characteristics displayed by believers, who will fall away, in the latter times. Notice that the scripture states, that these believers will no longer endure sound doctrine. These believers will follow after false prophets, who fabricate false visions and dreams, that they claim to have seen. They will follow after false teachers, who only proclaim certain truths in God's word, and give motivational talks, rather than teaching the full counsel of God. The false prophets and teachers, who teach these destructive heresies, will do so mainly for financial gain. Many of the false prophets and teachers, would have themselves, once been followers of the Lord. But over time, they will give more and more heed to deceiving spirits and doctrines of demons, thus not only deceiving others, but becoming more deceived themselves.

> *2 Peter 2:1-3 "But there were also false prophets among the people, even as there will be false teachers among you, who will secretly bring in destructive heresies, even denying the Lord who bought them, and bring on themselves swift destruction. (2) And many will follow their destructive ways, because of whom the way of truth will be blasphemed. (3) By covetousness they will exploit you with deceptive words; for a long time, their judgment has not been idle, and their destruction does not slumber."*

Again, in the above passage of scripture, the Holy Spirit gives us further insight regarding the false prophets and teachers, that will arise in the church in the last days. The Holy Spirit tells us that because of these individuals, the way of truth will be blasphemed. In other words, their destructive heresies and lifestyles, practiced in the name of Christianity, will convince many unbelievers that Christianity is for hypocrites, and therefore the gospel message cannot be believed. The Holy Spirit goes on to tell us, that because of covetousness, these individuals will exploit the church with deceptive words. In other words, their main motivation will be financial gain, and nothing else. Notice that Peter states, that they will bring in destructive heresies, "even" denying the Lord who bought them. That word "even", indicates that not all who bring in these destructive heresies, will deny the Lord that bought them. Nevertheless, the doctrines that they will teach, will lead those who follow them, into destruction. There will however, also be false prophets and teachers who have never known the Lord, and will be secretly brought in, to mislead the church (Galatians 2:4). These also, will lead many astray from following the Lord.

Let me illustrate by means of an example, to show just how close the church has come to the event called, the falling away. I was at a Christian men's breakfast, and I was led of the Lord to speak along this line. I knew of a brother in the audience, whose church was looking for a pastor. As one of the elders in that church, he was part of their board, that were interviewing potential candidates. So, in front of everyone, I asked him if his church was still looking for a pastor to fill their vacancy. And He obviously replied that they were. I then asked him if their board, in considering candidates for the position, would question those candidates as to what their core beliefs were. In other words, what their personal statement of faith was. My brother in the Lord, answered that they most definitely look at what the individual believes, when they consider candidates. I said that I would then like to hypothetically, apply for the position. And as part of my resume, I would give him three of the core beliefs that I held. And after I had given these statements of faith, would he give an answer as to whether I would be considered for the position, of pastor for their church. To which he agreed. I then proceeded to give him my statements of faith. I said, "Firstly, if I am to be pastor of your church, I will never preach that salvation through Jesus Christ is the only way to get to heaven, because I just don't believe that to be the truth. Secondly, if I am to be pastor of your church I will never mention the devil, hell, or sin, from the pulpit. And I will admonish the congregation, not to mention them either. And then thirdly, I need you to know, that I believe that Mormons are Christians, because they believe in Jesus". I then asked my brother, if I would be considered for their vacant pastor's position? To which he loudly replied, "No way"! At this point, all in the audience, also loudly agreed with him. I then told them that the current pastor, of the largest church in America, has publicly stated that each one of these statements form part of his core beliefs, and they are on public record for everyone to see. Most in the audience, still did not know who I was referring to, although by this time, some had caught on. And so, I named the pastor of the largest church in America. Most in the audience, were shocked to hear this. But the point was very clearly made. None in the audience, could accept that it was possible for someone with those beliefs, to even be considered for the role of deacon. And yet this person, who has stated each one of those beliefs in public, is the pastor of the largest church in America. And so, we find that we are very far advanced into the timeline, of the falling away occurring in the church.

A false prophet, is one who deceitfully claims, to have had visions and dreams from the Lord. They proclaim their visions, to attract attention to themselves and their ministries, mainly for financial gain, i.e. covetousness. The Holy Spirit through the apostle Paul, told us to test all things, including prophesies (1 Thessalonians 5:21). We test prophesies against scripture, to see if the prophecy given, lines up with God's word. We test visions and dreams, in the same manner. There are two very prominent ministers in the church today, who both recount fabricated visions, that they claim to have received from the Lord Jesus. Combined, these two ministers have over one million followers in the church today. And yet, the claimed visions of both men, when tested against scripture, are clearly proven to be false.

When Satan tries to deceive the church, he always disguises his lies, with an element of truth.

Genesis 3:4-5 "Then the serpent said to the woman, "You will not surely die. (5) For God knows that in the day you eat of it your eyes will be opened, and you will be like God, knowing good and evil."

In the above passage of scripture, we see that when Satan deceived Eve, he disguised his lie, with the truth. The truth he shared with Eve was, *"in the day you eat of it your eyes will be opened, and you will be like God, knowing good and evil"*. We know this was true, because that is exactly what happened. For after they ate the fruit, God said, "the man has become like one of Us, to know good and evil" (Genesis 3:22). The lie that Satan mixed with the truth however, was, *"you will not surely die"*. We know this was the lie, because the exact opposite happened. For after they ate the fruit, they both died in spirit. And so, as Satan deceived Eve, he continues to apply the same principle in the church today. Both men that I have mentioned earlier, as proclaiming false visions, also proclaim a number of truths, from the gospel. And because of this, they are able to mix their lies with the truth, thus deceiving many in the church. Sadly, there are some mature believers, that continue to listen to these ministries, even though they know these men's visions are completely false. Their view, is that because there is also truth that these ministries preach, that we should just ignore the false, and listen to the truth they proclaim. What they fail to realise however, is that while they may have the discernment to recognise what is true and what is false, baby believers do not have that same level of discernment. And because baby believers observe the mature believers listening to these ministries, they assume that everything they teach, is the truth. Do not misunderstand me, I am not speaking about ministries that are simply teaching error, because they have not yet learnt to rightly divided the word of truth. I am speaking about men, who are deliberately lying to the church. These practices should not be tolerated in the church, and mature believers who knowingly tolerate these ministries, run the risk of sinning against their Lord, as the apostle Paul mentions in the following passage of scripture. This is not something to be taken lightly.

1 Corinthians 8:11-12 "And because of your knowledge shall the weak brother perish, for whom Christ died? (12) But when you thus sin against the brethren, and wound their weak conscience, you sin against Christ."

The false teachers, are the ones who refuse to teach sound doctrine, by teaching the full counsel of God. They will only ever teach, one or two main truths from God's word, and then they will teach those truths, to the extreme. For example, you will never hear them teach on judgement, and the Lord's chastening, or any other "unpopular" subjects in the new testament. They will go to great lengths, to avoid teaching the full counsel of God. Even to the point, of denying that certain parts of the new testament, are for the church today. They are forced to do that, because the sections they deny, expose their teachings, as being false. Again, it is mainly for financial gain, i.e. covetousness, that they teach only that which is popular. Two of the most prominent ministers in the church today, who refuse to teach sound doctrine, by teaching the full counsel of God, have a combined following of almost nineteen million believers. One of those ministers, is the pastor I mentioned earlier, who refuses to teach the church about sin, hell, and the devil. The other minister, teaches the message of grace to such an extreme, that he denies the teaching our Lord Jesus gave on the subject of forgiveness for example, by stating, that Jesus was teaching the Jews on the subject, and not His church. As I have already mentioned, the false teachers are forced to deny certain parts of the new testament, because it exposes their teachings as being false. I have mentioned just four prominent ministers, who between themselves, have nearly twenty million followers in the church today. Now it may be, that the Lord will still grant these men repentance, so that they may come to their senses, and begin to teach the full counsel of God. But for now, these men are teaching a distorted, and in some cases dishonest, gospel. There are others also, that can be mentioned, all of whom have substantial followings in the church today. Because their doctrines are not sound, those who continue to follow them, run the risk of eventually falling away from following the Lord Jesus.

2 Timothy 3:1-9 "But know this, that in the last days perilous times will come: (2) For men will be lovers of themselves, lovers of money, ..., lovers of pleasure rather than lovers of God, (5) having a form of godliness but denying its power. And from such people turn away! (6) For of this sort are those who creep into households and make captives of gullible women loaded down with sins, ... (8) ... these also resist the truth: men of corrupt minds, disapproved concerning the faith; (9) but they will progress no further, for their folly will be manifest to all, as theirs also was."

You will recall that our Lord Jesus taught us, that we would know false prophets and false teachers, by their fruits (Matthew 7:16). In the above passage of scripture, the Holy Spirit gives us some characteristics, of ministries that should be avoided, in the last days. For in this passage, He clearly admonishes us, to turn away from these individuals. We know that the Holy Spirit is referring to ministries, for He tells us that these individuals make captives of households, including gullible women. The scripture tells us that these ministries resist the truth of God's word. In other words, these ministries preach and teach a distorted gospel. The first characteristic listed, are ministries that focus on the individual, and not on God. For notice that He says that these ministries promote love for oneself, and not love for God. The second characteristic listed, are ministries that focus on financial prosperity. The scripture plainly teaches us, that it is God's will that His people prosper financially. However, it is not God's will, that His people become covetous. The ministries that are to be avoided, are the ones that take the prosperity message to the extreme, and eventually become lovers of money, and lovers of pleasure, more than lovers of God. You will recall that the scripture teaches us, that the love of money, is the root of all evil (1 Timothy 6:10). The main thrust of their gospel message is, "it's all about me", and "what God can do for me?". It's not at all a message, of serving God, serving His body, and seeking to please Him. Remember that I started this section, by stating that God's word is always balanced. God does want to bless us, but He does that, so that we can be a blessing to others. For our Lord

The branch is becoming tender

Jesus, has taught us that it is more blessed to give, than to receive. And then the third characteristic listed, are ministries that have a form of godliness, but deny its power. All four, of the ministry examples that I have quoted earlier, have no power of God manifested through them. It is all man's wisdom. Now, more than ever before, false prophets and false teachers, have risen to prominent positions in the church. Pastors of churches, must be vigilant to protect their flocks in this hour, and warn those intrusted to their care, about false ministries. The Lord's shepherds who know His word, can very quickly expose false visions, and extreme teachings, for what they are, by showing that they are contrary to God's written word, and are thus able to protect the flocks that the Lord Jesus has placed into their care. Sadly, not all shepherds can rightly divide the word of truth, and are thus themselves vulnerable to being deceived, which leaves their flocks just as vulnerable. Sadly, the church today, is ripe for the event, called the falling away. All that is needed for that to happen, is the catalyst that will trigger that falling away to occur.

Matthew 24:9-16 "Then they will deliver you up to tribulation and kill you, and you will be hated by all nations for My name's sake. (10) And then many will be offended, will betray one another, and will hate one another. (11) Then many false prophets will rise up and deceive many. (12) And because lawlessness will abound, the love of many will grow cold. (13) But he who endures to the end shall be saved. (14) And this gospel of the kingdom will be preached in all the world as a witness to all the nations, and then the end will come. (15) "Therefore, when you see the 'Abomination of

The branch is becoming tender

Desolation,' spoken of by Daniel the prophet, standing in the holy place" (whoever reads, let him understand), (16) "then let those who are in Judea flee to the mountains."

As I have already mentioned at the start of this section, since the church began, there have always been those who have fallen away from following the Lord. And that will continue, as we draw closer to the end of the age. But we also read earlier, about an event, the Holy Spirit called, "the falling away" (2 Thessalonians 2:3). In other words, there is coming a time, when a significant number of believers will fall away from following the Lord Jesus. In the above quoted passage of scripture, our Lord Jesus spoke about this same event. For notice, that He states that there is coming a time, when many will be, "offended". When our Lord states, that many will be offended, He is referring to those, who will fall away from the faith. For in the parable of the sower, He used the same word to describe those who fell away (Matthew 13:21). So, what will be the cause, for such an event to occur in the church? Our Lord answers that question for us in this same passage, for He tells us that there is coming a time when the saints will be delivered up to tribulation, and to be killed, and they will be hated by all nations for His name's sake. In other words, our Lord is telling us that it is because of persecution, that many will become offended, i.e. they will fall away. Saints that are not grounded in the truth of God's word, and have been listening to a superficial gospel message, will very quickly become offended, when they find themselves being persecuted for the sake of the gospel. For example, there is a false teaching in some parts of the church today, that teaches that the church will rise up to take control of the world, and then deliver the world to the Lord, when He returns. You can readily see how the Christians that believe that lie, will become offended, when the exact opposite happens, i.e. they are given over to persecution by the world, rather than ruling over it. Another example, of a false teaching that will contribute to the falling away, is the teaching that the church will be "raptured", before the great tribulation takes place in the earth. Again, you can readily see that those who have been taught that they would be raptured before that event, will become offended, when they find themselves being subjected to that event.

Daniel 7:21-25 "I was watching; and the same horn was making war against the saints, and prevailing against them, ... (25) He shall speak pompous words against the Most High, shall persecute the saints of the Most High, And shall intend to change times and law. Then the saints shall be given into his hand for a time and times and half a time."

So, when will the event, called the falling away, occur? As we read earlier, when the apostle Paul referred to the falling away, he linked it to the revelation of the son of perdition. In the passage of scripture quoted earlier, our Lord Jesus also links the event of many becoming offended, with the revelation of the "Abomination of Desolation". The Abomination of Desolation that our Lord speaks of, refers to the event of the Anti-Christ sitting in the temple of God. The passage of scripture quoted above, refers specifically to the Anti-Christ, and his period of reign on the earth. But I want to draw your attention, to the fact that the scripture reveals to us that the Anti-

The branch is becoming tender

Christ will make war against the saints, and that he will prevail against them. In other words, he will be the cause of great persecution breaking out against the saints. And the scripture tells us that the saints will be given into his hands, for a period of three and half years. It will be during this period of great persecution, that two things will happen among the saints. Many will become offended, and fall away, while many others will remain faithful to the Lord, even to the point of martyrdom. Those who become offended and fall away, will be the saints who have not been grounded in the word of truth, and so will be unprepared for this period of intense persecution.

> *Revelation 13:4-7 "So they worshiped the dragon who gave authority to the beast; and they worshiped the beast, saying, "Who is like the beast? Who is able to make war with him?" (5) And he was given a mouth speaking great things and blasphemies, and he was given authority to continue for forty-two months. (6) Then he opened his mouth in blasphemy against God, to blaspheme His name, His tabernacle, and those who dwell in heaven. (7) It was granted to him to make war with the saints and to overcome them. And authority was given him over every tribe, tongue, and nation."*

The above passage of scripture refers to the Anti-Christ. In this passage, the Holy Spirit reveals to us the same truth, that was revealed to the prophet Daniel, i.e. the Anti-Christ will be allowed to reign on the earth for a period of three and a half years, and when he does reign, he will make war with the Lord's saints, and he will overcome them. In other words, he will institute great persecution against the Lord's saints. And so, it is more than likely, that it is during this period of intense persecution, that the falling away will occur. But even though the event of the falling away, will most probably occur when the Anti-Christ begins to reign on the earth, the seeds of that falling away, are already being sown in the church today. For, the saints who are not enduring sound doctrine today, will very quickly fall away, during the period of persecution, that the church is destined to go through. But also, as we draw closer to that time of intense persecution, there will be a gradual increase globally, of persecution against the church. And in fact, that trend has already begun.

In early November of this year, German Chancellor Angela Merkel, declared that Christianity is "the most persecuted religion in the world." Recent research confirms Merkel's claim — we may not want to hear it, but Christianity is in peril, like no other religion. Research shows that "Christians are targeted more than any other body of believers." It is reported that "200 million Christians (10 percent of the global total) are socially disadvantaged, harassed, or actively oppressed for their beliefs." Christianity is facing elimination in its Biblical homeland. Between a half and two-thirds of Christians in the Middle East, have departed or been killed over the past century. The intolerance and violence towards Christians, can be attributed to the rising Islamicization of Middle Eastern countries. Some of the oppression is government sanctioned and some government permitted; most is government ignored[8]. Recently, the Christian persecution advocacy group Open Doors, announced its annual list of 50 countries where it's hardest to be a Christian. The majority of the countries are in the Middle East, Sub-Saharan Africa, and South and Southeast

Asia. The list scores each country in terms in five quality-of-life areas and also looks at religiously motivated violence. For the third year in a row, the scores have gone up, clearly suggesting that persecution against Christians has increased worldwide. The group said the increase in incidents considered persecution, was alarming and only getting worse. They reported that persecution has increased again in 2016, and that they are the worst levels of persecution in modern times. They have gone on to report that the spread of persecution is now hitting nearly every continent in the world[9]. There is coming a time when more and more Christians, will be faced with having to give up everything, to follow Christ. There are many believers today, that are not willing to give up their favourite TV programme, to attend a prayer meeting. How are those believers going to cope with the persecution that is coming? Our Lord Jesus said they wouldn't cope, for He said that there is coming a time when, "you will be hated by all nations for My name's sake. And then many will be offended."

Matthew 24:12-13 "And because lawlessness will abound, the love of many will grow cold. (13) But he who endures to the end shall be saved."

But there is another influence, that will cause the falling away to occur in the last days, and that is the influence of lawlessness, that will increase in the earth. For as quoted in the above passage of scripture, our Lord said that, "because lawlessness will abound, the love of many will grow cold". When our Lord made this comment, He was referring to the love of believers, and not the love of those in the world. For the word translated "love" in this passage, is the Greek word "agape", referring to the love of God, that has been poured into the hearts of believers. In other words, our Lord was saying that many believers, will experience their love for God, growing cold, in the last days. Our Lord said that the reason this would happen, is because lawlessness would abound. Most have thought, that our Lord was referring to an increase in crime in the earth, that would cause the love of the saints to grow cold. But although there is an element of truth in that interpretation, that is not really what our Lord was referring to in this passage of scripture, for whenever scripture refers to "lawlessness", it refers to sin, because lawlessness is sin (1 John 3:4). In other words, our Lord was teaching us, that because sin will abound in the last days, that the love for God, of many believers, will grow cold. So why will an increase of sin in the world, affect the believers love for God? The definition of sin, is disobedience to God's laws. And so, as this world becomes more and more "liberal", they are actually becoming more and more, sinful. In other words, norms in society, are becoming more and more diametrically opposed, to God's laws. This environment, places believers in a situation, where they are forced to make a choice. Do they continue to obey God's laws, and thus become more and more offensive to society, or do they begin to abandon God's laws, in favour of being accepted by society? Also, for Christians to speak against sinful practices, will be to speak against what society calls, normal, and therefore, it is the Christian, who will find themselves, outside of "normal" society. As a result, many believers will not be able to endure that stigma, and so will rather back down on their Christian beliefs. And so, when faced with obeying God, and not condoning such acts, many Christians will in fact, support such acts, and thus find themselves joining the world, and opposing God. Many churches, and many influential leaders of those churches, will hold that view, and in fact we are already seeing that taking place, even in the church today. This is where many believers, then begin to allow their love for God, to grow cold. For their love for the world, begins to out-way, their love for God. And so, the way that they justify their decision, is to proclaim that they are actually walking in love, by not offending others. And on the surface, that seems like a good justification for their actions. For they proclaim that they do not want to offend people, but rather show them the love of God, for God is love, and by doing so, God will eventually change them. However, that argument is a distorted view of God's love, for God never ignores a person's sin, because He doesn't want to offend them. The whole ministry of the Holy Spirit, in the earth today, is to convict the world of sin, righteousness, and judgement (John 16:8). The reason He does that, is so that unbelievers can repent, and be saved. However, if believers refuse to proclaim God's laws, because society finds His laws offensive, how is it possible for the Holy Spirit to be able to convict the world of sin? And so, what happens is that the world continues in sin, because the Christians don't want to upset them. And the real reason Christians don't want to offend the world, is because they love the world, more than they love God. And so, we see, that because sin will abound, the love toward God, of many believers, will grow cold. One of the evidences of a believer's love for God, is their willingness to keep His commandments. Our Lord Jesus said it this way, "If you love Me, keep My commandments" (John 14:15). Believers that allow their love of God to grow cold, run the risk of eventually falling away from the Lord, altogether. Nevertheless, for those believers that choose to keep the Lord's commandments, they will begin to experience more and more hatred, in the last days. Which is why our Lord said that in the last days, that Christians will be hated by all nations, for His name's sake. Because even in nations, where believers are not persecuted because of their religious beliefs, because "freedom of religion" is allowed in those nations, Christians will be hated, because they will proclaim God's laws, which those societies will find offensive. This is why our Lord said, that only those who endure to the end, shall be saved.

I will close off this section by recounting a dream that the Lord gave me in 2014. In my dream, I was in an auditorium listening to a prophet of the Lord teaching the word of God. Who he was, I do not know. Two men were seated to my left, and just behind me. While the prophet of the Lord was teaching, these two men constantly spoke to each other in whispers. They spoke just loud enough for it to be a distraction to the Lord's minister, as he preached the word. Eventually the distraction became too much, and the prophet stopped his message. He faced the two men and confronted them to share with the rest of us, what they were whispering about. The two men refused to share what they were whispering about. The prophet then said to them that they were not whispering against him, but against God. At this saying, the two men became very angry, got up, and stormed out of the auditorium. Then across the auditorium, more and more people became upset and angry, and they too started to leave the auditorium. As they were leaving, the prophet said to them that they did not have to leave, but that it was their choice and that they could leave if that was their decision. My dream ended there. This dream that Lord gave me is for our day. In my dream, the two men who were whispering represent the false prophets and teachers who are constantly trying to undermine the message of the full counsel of God, from being taught. Over the coming years there will be more and more of God's ministers who will stand up and publicly challenge these men, regarding the distorted gospel that they are teaching. When that confrontation takes place, those men will be exposed for the false prophets and teachers that they are. For the kingdom of God is not in word, but in power. But even though they will be exposed, many will still follow them, and will thus ultimately fall away from following the Lord.

Chapter 3
The leaves are starting to show

The ten kings revealed

Daniel 7:7-24 "After this I saw in the night visions, and behold, a fourth beast, dreadful and terrible, exceedingly strong. It had huge iron teeth; it was devouring, breaking in pieces, and trampling the residue with its feet. It was different from all the beasts that were before it, and it had ten horns. (8) I was considering the horns, and there was another horn, a little one, coming up among them, before whom three of the first horns were plucked out by the roots. And there, in this horn, were eyes like the eyes of a man, and a mouth speaking pompous words. ... (19) "Then I wished to know the truth about the fourth beast, which was different from all the others, exceedingly dreadful, with its teeth of iron and its nails of bronze, which devoured, broke in pieces, and trampled the residue with its feet; (20) and the ten horns that were on its head, and the other horn which came up, before which three fell, namely, that horn which had eyes and a mouth which spoke pompous words, whose appearance was greater than his fellows. ... (23) "Thus he said: 'The fourth beast shall be A fourth kingdom on earth, which shall be different from all other kingdoms, and shall devour the whole earth, trample it and break it in pieces. (24) The ten horns are ten kings Who shall arise from this kingdom. And another shall rise after them; He shall be different from the first ones, and shall subdue three kings."

      The above passage of scripture, reveals to us the fourth kingdom that will be in the earth, when our Lord Jesus returns. We have already seen in an earlier section of this teaching, that the fourth kingdom referred to in Daniel's dream, is in fact the religion of Islam. In this section, we want to concentrate on the ten horns that Daniel saw in his dream. In giving us the interpretation to the dream, the angel tells us that the ten horns are in fact, ten kings. I want you to notice that in God's sequence of events, that these ten kings, will arise or emerge if you will, from within the fourth kingdom. Because we have already identified the fourth kingdom as being the religion of Islam, it is self-evident that these ten kings will be a confederacy of ten leaders, that will emerge from within the world's Islamic states. Something else of importance, that needs to be mentioned here, is that because the fourth kingdom has been identified as the religion of Islam, it is more than likely, that the ten leaders will be religious leaders of Islam, i.e. Grand Muftis and Grand Ayatollahs, rather than secular leaders of nations states. The little horn referred to in Daniel's dream, before whom three of the first horns were plucked out by the roots, refers to the Anti-Christ himself. And so, we see that ultimately, the Anti-Christ will also arise from within the religion of Islam. But we will not look at the Anti-Christ in any detail in this section however, as we want to concentrate on what scripture reveals to us, about these ten leaders. From this passage of scripture, we see that not long after these ten leaders arise, that three of them will in fact, be subdued by the Anti-Christ himself. In connection with the three being subdued by the Anti-

Christ, it is interesting to note that the religion of Islam has two main streams, i.e. Sunni and Shi'a. The majority of Islamic states are mainly Sunni, but there are three Islamic states today, that are mainly Shi'a. Those states are, Iran, Iraq and Lebanon. It is well known that the followers of the two streams of Islam, have clashed violently in the past, and continue to do so, even today. And so, it is very possible that when the Anti-Christ is revealed in the earth, that these three mainly Shi'a Islamic states, will be brought into the Sunni fold.

Revelation 17:1-14 "Then one of the seven angels who had the seven bowls came and talked with me, saying to me, "Come, I will show you the judgment of the great harlot who sits on many waters, (2) with whom the kings of the earth committed fornication, and the inhabitants of the earth were made drunk with the wine of her fornication." (3) So, he carried me away in the Spirit into the wilderness. And I saw a woman sitting on a scarlet beast which was full of names of blasphemy, having seven heads and ten horns. ... (6) I saw the woman, drunk with the blood of the saints and with the blood of the martyrs of Jesus. And when I saw her, I marveled with great amazement. (7) But the angel said to me, "Why did you marvel? I will tell you the mystery of the woman and of the beast that carries her, which has the seven heads and the ten horns. ... (12) "The ten horns which you saw are ten kings who have received no kingdom as yet, but they receive authority for one hour as kings with the beast. (13) These are of one mind, and they will give their power and authority to the beast. (14) These will make war with the Lamb, and the Lamb will overcome them, for He is Lord of lords and King of kings; and those who are with Him are called, chosen, and faithful."

The next time we see the ten kings mentioned in scripture, is in the vision given to the apostle John. In the above passage of scripture, the Lord gives us some more insight into who these ten leaders are, and what they will do, at the end of the age. Firstly, we see that their reign will be relatively brief, because the scripture says that they receive authority for one hour, as kings. When we discuss the Anti-Christ in a later section, we will see that he will rule the fourth kingdom, for at least seven years. And because the ten kings will be in place, before the Anti-Christ is manifested in the earth, it is self-evident that the reign of the ten kings, will be for a period longer than seven years. Secondly, we see that they will form a confederacy, because the scripture says that they will be of one mind. And then thirdly, we see that they will align themselves with the Anti-Christ, when he is manifested in the earth, because the scripture says that they will give their power and authority to the beast, who is the Anti-Christ. Because these leaders will align themselves with the Anti-Christ, they will form the nucleus of the nations, that will stand against the Lord Jesus at the battle of Armageddon (Revelation 16:16). For the scripture says that these ten, will make war with the Lamb, and the Lamb will overcome them, for He is Lord of lords and King of kings.

Psalms 83:1-8 "Do not keep silent, O God! Do not hold Your peace, and do not be still, O God! (2) For behold, Your enemies make a tumult; And those who hate You have lifted up their head. (3) They have taken crafty counsel against Your people, and consulted together against Your sheltered ones. (4) They have said, "Come, and let us cut them off from being a nation, That the name of Israel may be remembered no more." (5) For they have consulted together with one consent; They form a confederacy against You: (6) The tents of Edom and the Ishmaelites; Moab and the Hagrites; (7) Gebal, Ammon, and Amalek; Philistia with the inhabitants of Tyre; (8) Assyria also has joined with them; They have helped the children of Lot."

Because the confederacy of the Islamic states will be aligned to the Anti-Christ, they will be used by him, to invade the nation of Israel. It will be at that time, that the Anti-Christ will set up his three-and-a-half-year reign, from the temple, in the city Jerusalem. The above passage of scripture, reveals to us ten nations, that will constitute this confederacy. Each of the nations listed in this passage, equate geographically, to the Islamic nations that surround Israel today. Notice that the scripture teaches us that they will form a confederacy, and that their stated aim, is to cut off Israel from being a nation, so that Israel may be remembered no more. Islam has the exact same stated aim, for the Qur'an is replete with verses that can be described only, as virulently anti-Semitic. One of the more enlightening passages, is in their Sahih al-Bukhari Book 52, Hadith 177, where it is recorded that Allah's apostle said, "The Day of Judgment will not have come until you fight with the Jews, and the stones and the trees behind which a Jew will be hiding will say: 'O Muslim! There is a Jew hiding behind me, come and kill him!'" We will examine in more detail; what scripture says about the event of the invasion of Israel, in a later section.

The leaves are starting to show

Revelation 17:15-18 "Then he said to me, "The waters which you saw, where the harlot sits, are peoples, multitudes, nations, and tongues. (16) And the ten horns which you saw on the beast, these will hate the harlot, make her desolate and naked, eat her flesh and burn her with fire. (17) For God has put it into their hearts to fulfill His purpose, to be of one mind, and to give their kingdom to the beast, until the words of God are fulfilled. (18) And the woman whom you saw is that great city which reigns over the kings of the earth."

The above passage of scripture, teaches us that it is the ten leaders that will hate the harlot, make her desolate and naked, eat her flesh, and burn her with fire. For God has put it into their hearts, to fulfill His purpose. As we will see in a later section, the harlot, which is also called "Babylon the great" in scripture (Revelation 17:5), refers to this world's system, with all its wealth. And so, we see that it will be these ten leaders, that will be instrumental in bringing about the complete destruction of the world's economies, and almost overnight, completely erasing the wealth of multitudes. But I want you to notice, that in the above passage of scripture, that the angel reveals to us that all ten horns, would be instrumental in orchestrating the destruction of the harlot. In the vision of the ten horns, given to the prophet Daniel, we saw that when the Anti-Christ is manifested in the earth, that three of the horns will be plucked out by the roots. And so, we see from this passage, that before the Anti-Christ is manifested in the earth, and before they join with him, to invade the nation of Israel, that one of the first things that these ten leaders will do, is that they will be used by God,

The leaves are starting to show

to destroy the harlot, for the scripture says that, "God has put it into *their hearts* to fulfill His purpose". In the following section, we will discuss just how these leaders will destroy the world's system. But in this section, we want to concentrate on how it is possible, that these ten leaders will be able to orchestrate such a destructive event in the earth, and not be held to account. For if this act of global destruction, were to be taken by leaders of nation states, then there would be quick and decisive retribution, taken by the rest of the world, against those nation states. However, scripture plainly reveals, that no retribution occurs after the world's system is destroyed by these ten leaders, for these same leaders continue to reign with the Anti-Christ, until the end of the age. So why is that? The reason is, because it will not be secular leaders of nation states, that will instigate the destruction of the harlot.

To understand how this is possible, we can look at examples of recent acts of terrorism, that have occurred in cities around the world, in the name of Islam. Even though many of the nations, in which these acts of terrorism took place, have powerful armies, those same armies were powerless to act, because there was no nation state that was responsible, against which those armies could act. In the same manner, these ten leaders will orchestrate the destruction of the world's economies, in the name of Islam. Someone will say, that when Osama bin Laden, orchestrated the destruction of the twin towers, on 11th September 2001, that the United States invaded the nation of Afghanistan, in retribution. The reason that the United States invaded that nation, was because Afghanistan was harbouring Osama bin Laden at the time, and they refused to deliver him up for prosecution. But this time it will be different, because although Osama bin Laden was idolized by many

Muslims, he was not one of their religious leaders. And so, this time, the world will be powerless to take retribution, because to do so, would require them to act against the whole religion of Islam. And as we have already seen in a previous section, Islam will account for one quarter of the world's population, by that time. Also, it will be very soon after the event of the destruction of the harlot, that the Anti-Christ will be revealed in the earth, and so by that time, it will be too late for the world to take any acts of retribution against the ten leaders, for they will be under the protection of the Anti-Christ, so to speak. Nevertheless, scripture is clear, when it states that it will be the ten leaders (of Islam), that will orchestrate the destruction of the harlot. Someone will ask, why it is that these ten Muslim leaders would want to destroy the world's economies, because surely in destroying it, they will negatively affect their own people. In answer to that question, we can look at the motivation of terror attacks, on the world today. As an example, it is estimated that in 2014 alone (and the trend has not changed since then), about 30,000 people were killed in terror attacks worldwide. The vast majority of those perpetrating the violence were Muslim, but so were the victims. In other words, of the approximately 30,000 dead, the vast majority were Muslims. That's crucial to understand, because it sheds light on the question, of why these Muslim leaders will want to destroy the world's system. Islamic terrorists don't just hate America or the West. They hate the modern world, and they particularly hate Muslims, who are trying to live in the modern world[10]. And so, it is that hatred, that will motivate these leaders to destroy the world system, that we know today. That hatred is spiritual in its origin, and we have already seen in scripture, that God Himself, has put it into their hearts to fulfill His purpose, and bring about the judgement of the great harlot.

The destruction of Babylon

Revelation 17:1-18 "Then one of the seven angels who had the seven bowls came and talked with me, saying to me, "Come, I will show you the judgment of the great harlot who sits on many waters, (2) with whom the kings of the earth committed fornication, and the inhabitants of the earth were made drunk with the wine of her fornication." (3) So, he carried me away in the Spirit into the wilderness. And I saw a woman sitting on a scarlet beast which was full of names of blasphemy, having seven heads and ten horns. (4) The woman was arrayed in purple and scarlet, and adorned with gold and precious stones and pearls, having in her hand a golden cup full of abominations and the filthiness of her fornication. (5) And on her forehead a name was written: MYSTERY, BABYLON THE GREAT, THE MOTHER OF HARLOTS AND OF THE ABOMINATIONS OF THE EARTH. (6) I saw the woman, drunk with the blood of the saints and with the blood of the martyrs of Jesus. And when I saw her, I marveled with great amazement. (7) But the angel said to me, "Why did you marvel? I will tell you the mystery of the woman and of the beast that carries her, which has the seven heads and the ten horns. (8) The beast that you saw was, and is not, and will ascend out of the bottomless pit and go to perdition. And those who dwell on the earth will marvel, whose names are not written in the Book of Life from the foundation of the world, when they see the beast that was, and is not, and yet is. (9) "Here is the mind which has wisdom: The seven heads are seven mountains on which the woman sits. (10) There are also seven kings. Five have fallen, one is, and the other has not yet come. And when he comes, he must continue a short time. (11) The beast that was, and is not, is himself also the eighth, and is of the seven, and is going to perdition. (12) "The ten horns which you saw are ten kings who have received no kingdom as yet, but they receive authority for one hour as kings with the beast. (13) These are of one mind, and they will give their power and authority to the beast. (14) These will make war with the Lamb, and the Lamb will overcome them, for He is Lord of lords and King of kings; and those who are with Him are called, chosen, and faithful." (15) Then he said to me, "The waters which you saw, where the harlot sits, are peoples, multitudes, nations, and tongues. (16) And the ten horns which you saw on the beast, these will hate the harlot, make her desolate and naked, eat her flesh and burn her with fire. (17) For God has put it into their hearts to fulfill His purpose, to be of one mind, and to give their kingdom to the beast, until the words of God are fulfilled. (18) And the woman whom you saw is that great city which reigns over the kings of the earth."

In the above passage of scripture, we have already identified who the seven kings are, and we have identified who the ten kings are. In a later section, we will look in more detail, at the beast, who is called the Anti-Christ. But in this section, we want to have a look at the great harlot, referred to in the above passage of scripture, as "Babylon the great". The image of the harlot, given to us in this passage, shows the wealth and luxury of this world being displayed, for the scripture says that, "the woman was arrayed in purple and scarlet, and adorned with gold and precious stones and pearls." Not only do we see the luxury of this world on display, but we also see the sin of this world being displayed, for the scripture says that she held, "in her hand a golden cup full of abominations and the filthiness of her fornication". In other words, the Lord is revealing to His saints, what this world's system looks like, in the spirit. This passage also reveals further insights, to show us that the harlot represents this world's system, for the angel tells us that the seven heads, which represented the seven kings that we have already discussed, were seven mountains on which the woman sits. We have seen that the seven kings listed, started with king Nebuchadnezzar, who's reign began in 605 BC, and ended with the destruction of the Sasanian Empire in 651 AD. And so, we see that the harlot was present, throughout that period. But not only was she present, at the start of the reign of king Nebuchadnezzar, but she had been there long before king Nebuchadnezzar was manifested in the earth, for the scripture tells us that the woman was sitting on the beast, referring to the Anti-Christ. And as we will see, in the section when we look at the Anti-Christ, the Anti-Christ was present on the earth, long before the flood in Noah's time. And so, it is very clear, that the harlot has been present on the earth, throughout all the ages. It is also clear, that she is still present on the earth today, for the scripture says that the woman, still "reigns over the kings of the earth". Another clear indication given to us, to show us that Babylon the great, is in fact referring to this world's system, is that the waters where the harlot sits, are peoples, multitudes,

The leaves are starting to show

nations, and tongues. In other words, every nation on the earth, falls under the influence of the harlot, called Babylon the great.

Revelation 18:1-5 "After these things I saw another angel coming down from heaven, having great authority, and the earth was illuminated with his glory. (2) And he cried mightily with a loud voice, saying, "Babylon the great is fallen, is fallen, and has become a dwelling place of demons, a prison for every foul spirit, and a cage for every unclean and hated bird! (3) For all the nations have drunk of the wine of the wrath of her fornication, the kings of the earth have committed fornication with her, and the merchants of the earth have become rich through the abundance of her luxury." (4) And I heard another voice from heaven saying, "Come out of her, my people, lest you share in her sins, and lest you receive of her plagues. (5) For her sins have reached to heaven, and God has remembered her iniquities."

The above passage of scripture, introduces us to the judgement, that will be pronounced upon this world's system. Again, we see in this passage, that all the earth has shared in her sins, for the scripture says that, "all the nations have drunk of the wine of the wrath of her fornication". And again, we also see that Babylon the great, also represents the wealth and luxury of this world, for the scripture says that, "the merchants of the earth have become rich through the abundance of her luxury". The Lord Himself, also clearly reveals to us in this passage, that Babylon the great, refers to this world's system, for He warns His saints to, "come out of her, lest we share in her sins". When God tells us to come out of the world, He is not telling us to live in isolation from the world, but rather, that we are not to partake in the covetousness and sin, that is in the world.

2 Corinthians 6:16-17 "And what agreement has the temple of God with idols? For you are the temple of the living God. As God has said: "I will dwell in them and walk among them. I will be their God, and they shall be My people." (17) Therefore "Come out from among them and be separate, says the Lord. Do not touch what unclean, and I will receive you."

In the above passage of scripture, God uses almost the identical phrase, when He instructs His saints, to separate themselves from the world. For in the passage, when He referred to Babylon the great, He said, "Come out of her, my people, lest you share in her sins." In the above passage, when God is admonishing His saints, to live separated lives from the world, He says, "Come out from among them and be separate, says the Lord". Clearly, the Lord is referring to the same thing, when He speaks of the world, and when He speaks of Babylon the great.

1 Corinthians 5:9-10 "I wrote to you in my epistle not to keep company with sexually immoral people. (10) Yet I certainly did not mean with the sexually immoral people of this world, or with the covetous, or extortioners, or idolaters, since then you would need to go out of the world."

The leaves are starting to show

I stated earlier, that when God tells us to come out of the world, He is not telling us to live in isolation from the world, but rather, that we are not to partake in the covetousness and sin, that is in the world. The Holy Spirit, in the above passage of scripture, confirms that truth for us. For it is not the will of God, that His children should isolate themselves from the world, but rather, that we should live separated lives in the world, as light and salt, in the world. And so, when God tells us to come out of the world, He is telling us not to partake in the lusts and covetousness, that forms part of this world's system.

1 John 2:15-17 "Do not love the world or the things in the world. If anyone loves the world, the love of the Father is not in him. (16) For all that is in the world--the lust of the flesh, the lust of the eyes, and the pride of life--is not of the Father but is of the world. (17) And the world is passing away, and the lust of it; but he who does the will of God abides forever."

In the above passage of scripture, the Holy Spirit, through the apostle John, again confirms the truth to us, that we as believers, are to keep away from the lusts of this world. I want you to notice, that in describing the world, in this passage of scripture, that the Holy Spirit refers to, "the lust of the flesh, the lust of the eyes, and the pride of life". In other words, He is referring to the covetousness and sin, that is in the world. All the above passages of scripture, have confirmed for us, that Babylon the great, in fact, refers to the wealth, and luxury, and sin, that is in the world. And so, now that we have identified that Babylon the great is this world's system, we can more clearly understand the judgement, that will be pronounced upon her.

Revelation 18:6-24 "Render to her just as she rendered to you, and repay her double according to her works; in the cup which she has mixed, mix double for her. (7) In the measure that she glorified herself and lived luxuriously, in the same measure give her torment and sorrow; for she says in her heart, 'I sit as queen, and am no widow, and will not see sorrow.' (8) Therefore, her plagues will come in one day--death and mourning and famine. And she will be utterly burned with fire, for strong is the Lord God who judges her. (9) "The kings of the earth who committed fornication and lived luxuriously with her will weep and lament for her, when they see the smoke of her burning, (10) standing at a distance for fear of her torment, saying, 'Alas, alas, that great city Babylon, that mighty city! For in one hour your judgment has come.' (11) "And the merchants of the earth will weep and mourn over her, for no one buys their merchandise anymore: (12) merchandise of gold and silver, precious stones and pearls, fine linen and purple, silk and scarlet, every kind of citron wood, every kind of object of ivory, every kind of object of most precious wood, bronze, iron, and marble; (13) and cinnamon and incense, fragrant oil and frankincense, wine and oil, fine flour and wheat, cattle and sheep, horses and chariots, and bodies and souls of men. (14) The fruit that your soul longed for has gone from you, and all the things which are rich and splendid have gone from you, and you shall find them no more at all. (15) The merchants of these things, who became rich by her, will stand at a distance for fear of her torment, weeping and wailing, (16) and saying, 'Alas, alas, that great city that was clothed in fine linen, purple, and scarlet, and adorned with gold and precious stones and pearls! (17) For in one hour such great riches came to nothing.' Every shipmaster, all who travel by ship, sailors, and as many as trade on the sea, stood at a distance (18) and cried out when they saw the smoke of her burning, saying, 'What is like this great city?' (19) "They threw dust on their heads and cried out, weeping and wailing, and saying, 'Alas, alas, that great city, in which all who had ships on the sea became rich by her wealth! For in one hour she is made desolate.' (20) "Rejoice over her, O heaven, and you holy apostles and prophets, for God has avenged you on her!" (21) Then a mighty angel took up a stone like a great millstone and threw it into the sea, saying, "Thus with violence the great city Babylon shall be thrown down, and shall not be found anymore. (22) The sound of harpists, musicians, flutists, and trumpeters shall not be heard in you anymore. No craftsman of any craft shall be found in you anymore, and the sound of a millstone shall not be heard in you anymore. (23) The light of a lamp shall not shine in you anymore, and the voice of bridegroom and bride shall not be heard in you anymore. For your merchants were the great men of the earth, for by your sorcery all the nations were deceived. (24) And in her was found the blood of prophets and saints, and of all who were slain on the earth."

The above passage of scripture, gives us a vivid account, of the judgement to be incurred by Babylon the great. There are three main points, that the Holy Spirit reveals to us in this passage. Firstly, we see that her destruction will be very sudden, in that it will happen overnight. In other words, its destruction will not be gradual, but rather as a result of a sudden cataclysmic event taking place, which will take everyone by surprise. For the scripture states, that, "her plagues will come in one day", and "in one hour your judgment has come", and again, "in one hour such great riches came to nothing". Secondly, we see that her destruction will be extremely violent. For the scripture says, that, "a mighty angel took up a stone like a great millstone and threw it into the sea, saying, "Thus with violence the great city Babylon shall be thrown down, and shall not be found anymore". The scripture also gives us an indication, as to what type of violence will be used to destroy her, for the scripture says that, "she will be utterly burned with fire", and "they will see the smoke of her burning, standing at a distance for fear of her torment". It is interesting to note, that in describing those who see the smoke of her burning, that they will stand at a distance, for fear of her torment. The Holy Spirit records that aspect for us, on more than one occasion, for the scripture says, "the merchants of these things, who became rich by her, will stand at a distance for fear of her torment", and again, "every shipmaster, all who travel by ship, sailors, and as many as trade on the sea, stood at a distance and cried out when they saw the smoke of her burning". When we look at the instrument, that will be used to destroy Babylon the great, we will have a clearer understanding of why it is, that all who saw her burning, stood at a distance, for fear of her torment. And then finally, we see in this passage of scripture, just what it is, that will be destroyed on that day. For we see clearly, that it is the wealth of the world, that will be destroyed.

The leaves are starting to show

For the scripture says, "therefore, her plagues will come in one day--death and mourning and famine", and, "no one buys their merchandise anymore", and again, "the fruit that your soul longed for has gone from you, and all the things which are rich and splendid have gone from you, and you shall find them no more at all", and again, "for in one hour such great riches came to nothing". We also see in this passage, that it is mainly the world leaders, the business moguls, and those who were made rich with the wealth of the world, that will cry out weeping and wailing, on that day. For the scripture says that, it is the kings of the earth, who will weep and lament for her, and it is the merchants who became rich by her, that will stand at a distance for fear of her torment, weeping and wailing, and again, that her merchants, were the great men of the earth. It is these individuals, that will be greatly affected by the destruction of the harlot, but nevertheless, the whole world will feel the effects of her destruction.

We have seen in an earlier section, that it is the ten leaders of the Muslim faith, that will be instrumental in orchestrating the destruction of the world's economy. So how will they be able to accomplish such a thing? Currently, more and more Muslim nations are developing nuclear capabilities, for peaceful purposes. But there are also Muslim nations, that want to develop nuclear capabilities, for military purposes. Not forgetting the fact, that Pakistan, which is a Muslim nation, already has nuclear weapons. And it is no secret, that Muslim extremists have sought, and continue to seek, ways to get access to nuclear weapons. In his 2003 work, 'A Treatise on the Law of the Weapons of Mass Destruction Against the Unbelievers', one Saudi radical scholar argued that since roughly ten million Muslims had been killed by Americans, killing that same number of Americans was permissible, including through the use of weapons of mass destruction. Such a *fatwa* (an Islamic scholar's or clergyman's analysis on interpreting Islamic law) effectively provides a religious blank cheque for mass murder. Against this backdrop, statements by some Islamists, including religiously fervent physicists who maintain that Pakistan's nuclear weapons 'belong to all Muslims', acquire a new significance[11]. And so, we see that the door is slowly opening, for Muslim extremists, to be able to eventually gain access to nuclear weapons. When we look at the destruction of the harlot, as recorded in scripture, we see that, "she will be utterly burned with fire". It is common knowledge, that a nuclear explosion produces a deadly fireball at its core, which destroys all within its radius. The bible also speaks of all who travel by ship, and as many as trade on the sea, standing at a distance, and crying out when they see the smoke of her burning. Currently, the top ten financial centres of the world, are all cities that are built around sea ports. It is therefore not inconceivable, that those willing to martyr themselves for the Muslim faith, could set off nuclear devices in a co-ordinated attack, in the harbours of those cities, thus destroying those cities, and killing millions. The effect of just one 10-kiloton nuclear device detonating in one of these cities would destroy all buildings within a range of 500 metres, and instantly kill half a million people. Fire, debris and long-term radiation effects would drive the death toll to well over one million. The electromagnetic pulse created by a nuclear weapon, would have the added effect of causing significant damage to electronic equipment, on which the economies of the world have become thoroughly dependent[12].

You will recall, that earlier I commented on the fact that all who witnessed the burning of the harlot, stood at a distance, for fear of her torment. We all know, that one of the worst aspects of a nuclear explosion, is the radioactive fallout that occurs, as a result. This would explain why the scripture says, that those who watch the disaster unfold, will stand at a distance. The reason they will stand at a distance, is because they will not want to become contaminated with the radioactive fallout, produced by a nuclear explosion. If such a bomb was exploded in a major city, the long-term radiation effects would make entire parts of that city uninhabitable, causing enormous economic damage. Scripture plainly tells us, that it is the ten kings that arise from the fourth kingdom, that God will use, to destroy Babylon the great. And scripture also tells us, that they will destroy the harlot, by fire. The world has finally reached a stage, when for the first time, since God gave John this vision, it is entirely possible for this event to take place in the earth. Multiple nuclear detonations, would severely harm critical parts of the world's infrastructure, including banking and finance. The economic cost incurred by the United States, as a result of the co-ordinated, 11th September terrorist attacks in 2001, has been conservatively estimated at one trillion dollars. Obviously, a nuclear terrorist attack, would be exponentially greater, in cost. And multiple detonations, occurring at the same time in numerous cities, would be a cost that will cripple and destroy, the world's economy. I will end this section, with an excerpt of a vision of end time events, that the Lord Jesus gave to the prophet Kenneth E Hagin, in 1950, "I looked at the scroll again, and again I looked to see what I had read about. I saw the skyline of a large city. Looking closer, I saw the skyscrapers were burned-out hulls. Portions of the city lay in ruins. It was not written that just one city would be destroyed, burned and in ruins, but that there would be many such cities." The vision given to the Lord's prophet, certainly agrees with an event of multiple nuclear detonations taking place, in numerous cities around the world. And thus, Babylon the great will be destroyed by fire.

The two witnesses revealed

Romans 11:25-26 "For I do not desire, brethren, that you should be ignorant of this mystery, lest you should be wise in your own opinion, that blindness in part has happened to Israel until the fullness of the Gentiles has come in. (26) And so, all Israel will be saved, as it is written: "The Deliverer will come out of Zion, and He will turn away ungodliness from Jacob."

As we will see in this section, the primary purpose of the two witnesses being manifested in the earth in the last days, will be, to bring Israel to salvation. The two witnesses will not be sent to the gentiles, for not long before the two witnesses are manifested in the earth, the fullness of the gentiles would have come into the kingdom. Although, as we have seen in a previous section, as we draw closer to the end of the age, the number of Jewish believers will continue to steadily rise, nevertheless, by the time the two witnesses are manifested in the earth, the clear majority of Jews, will still not have accepted Jesus as their Messiah.

Malachi 4:5-6 "Behold, I will send you Elijah the prophet Before the coming of the great and dreadful day of the Lord. (6) And he will turn the hearts of the fathers to the children, And the hearts of the children to their fathers, Lest I come and strike the earth with a curse."

The above passage of scripture prophesied about two separate events. For in this passage, God promised Israel that He would send Elijah the prophet, to that nation, before the coming of the Lord. God fulfilled the first part of that prophecy, when our Lord came to the earth the first time. For we know that on that occasion, God sent His prophet John, in the spirit of Elijah. And we know that John was sent by God, to prepare the nation of Israel, for their coming Messiah. On that occasion, John was not sent to the world, he was only sent to the children of Israel. We know that our Lord is coming back to the earth again. And so, God will fulfil the second part of that prophecy, when our Lord comes to the earth the second time. When God sends His prophet this time, his mandate will remain the same as the first time. He will be sent by God, to the nation of Israel, to prepare them for their coming Messiah. And so, we see that on the second occasion, as on the first, the Lord's prophet will not be sent to the world, he will only be sent to the children of Israel. This time however, God will send the prophet Elijah himself, and not another prophet in the spirit of Elijah.

Matthew 17:10-13 "And His disciples asked Him, saying, "Why then do the scribes say that Elijah must come first?" (11) Jesus answered and said to them, "Indeed, Elijah is coming first and will restore all things. (12) But I say to you that Elijah has come already, and they did not know him but did to him whatever they wished. Likewise, the Son of Man is also about to suffer at their hands." (13) Then the disciples understood that He spoke to them of John the Baptist."

In the above passage of scripture, our Lord Jesus explained the truth to us, that Elijah came the first time, in the form of John the Baptist. It is important to note, that the ministry of John the Baptist, ushered in the kingdom of God on the earth. For Our Lord Jesus taught us that the law and the prophets were until John, and that from then onwards, the kingdom of God was proclaimed (Luke 16:16). Our Lord went on to teach us in the above passage, that once again, the prophet Elijah himself, will come to the earth. Notice, that our Lord teaches us that when Elijah comes this time, that his mandate remains the same, for he is mandated by God, to restore all things. When our Lord says that Elijah will restore all things, He is referring to the fact that Elijah will restore Israel as a nation, to their Messiah. Just as John's ministry brought the age of the law and the prophets to a close, so this time, Elijah's ministry will bring this current age, to a close. After Elijah is removed from the earth in that day, the gospel message will no longer be proclaimed in the earth. For it is immediately after that event, that the church will be removed from the earth, and the wrath of God will be poured out on the earth.

Revelation 11:3-13 "And I will give power to my two witnesses, and they will prophesy one thousand two hundred and sixty days, clothed in sackcloth." (4) These are the two olive trees and the two lampstands standing before the God of the earth. (5) And if anyone wants to harm them, fire proceeds from their mouth and devours their enemies. And if anyone wants to harm them, he must be killed in this manner. (6) These have power to shut heaven, so that no rain falls in the days of their prophecy; and they have power over waters to turn them to blood, and to strike the earth with all plagues, as often as they desire. (7) When they finish their testimony, the beast that ascends out of the bottomless pit will make war against them, overcome them, and kill them. (8) And their dead bodies will lie in the street of the great city which spiritually is called Sodom and Egypt, where also our Lord was crucified. (9) Then those from the peoples, tribes, tongues, and nations will see their dead bodies three-and-a-half days, and not allow their dead bodies to be put into graves. (10) And those who dwell on the earth will rejoice over them, make merry, and send gifts to one another, because these two prophets tormented those who dwell on the earth. (11) Now after the three-and-a-half days the breath of life from God entered them, and they stood on their feet, and great fear fell on those who saw them. (12) And they heard a loud voice from heaven saying to them, "Come up here." And they ascended to heaven in a cloud, and their enemies saw them. (13) In the same hour there was a great earthquake, and a tenth of the city fell. In the earthquake seven thousand people were killed, and the rest were afraid and gave glory to the God of heaven."

When God sends Elijah this time, He will send him with a second witness. These two witnesses will preach the gospel to the children of Israel, for a period of three-and-a-half-years. Unlike John the Baptist however, who's ministry did not demonstrate the power of God, the gift of the working of miracles, will be very prominent in the ministries of the two witnesses. Scripture reveals to us that their ministries will not only impact the nation of Israel however, but also the whole earth. For they will have power to strike the whole earth, with various plagues, as often as they desire. In fact, they will torment the earth to such a degree, that when they are finally killed, the earth will rejoice over the fact that they have been removed from the earth. So why is it, that God will allow these two men to strike the earth with various plagues, as often as they desire? The reason is, because the world would have changed dramatically, by the time the two witnesses are manifested in the earth. As I have already mentioned, the fullness of the gentiles would have come into the kingdom of God, and so no more salvations will take place in the nations of the world. The Anti-Christ would recently have invaded Israel with his armies, and put an end to the daily sacrifice in the temple. He would have also set himself up as god in the earth, and instituted great persecution against both the Jews, and the Lord's saints, in the nations under his control. As we have already seen in a previous section, it is during this time, that the falling away in the church, will take place. But it is also a time when many saints, who remain faithful to the Lord, will be martyred for their faith. It will be upon the nations that institute persecution against the Lord's saints, that the two witnesses will pronounce judgement, by striking those nations with the plagues, as mentioned in this passage of scripture. Because the two witnesses will be in direct opposition to the Anti-Christ, he will direct numerous assassination attempts, on the lives of the Lord's prophets. But as this passage of scripture reveals to us, those who do attempt to assassinate the Lord's prophets, will themselves be killed, with fire that proceeds from the prophet's mouths. However, as revealed to us in this passage of scripture, at the close of their ministry, the two prophets will confront the Anti-Christ himself, in the city of Jerusalem. In this confrontation, it is the Anti-Christ that will prevail, and he will kill the two prophets. The Anti-Christ will not allow their bodies to be buried, and their bodies will lie in the street of Jerusalem, for all the world to see. And the world will rejoice, to see that their god has overcome the prophets of the Lord. However, after three-and-half-days, God will raise up His prophets from the dead, and they will ascend into heaven. It is at that time that the remaining saints on the earth, will also be caught away from the earth. And so, the wrath of God will begin to be poured out on the earth, beginning with the great earthquake mentioned in this passage. Although at the end of their ministry, the two witnesses will be killed in the city of Jerusalem, they will not minister from that city, during their period on the earth. For just as John their forerunner, ministered to Israel in the wilderness, so these two men will also minister in the wilderness, when they are manifested in the earth.

Revelation 12:6-14 "Then the woman fled into the wilderness, where she has a place prepared by God, that they should feed her there one thousand two hundred and sixty days. ... (13) Now when the dragon saw that he had been cast to the earth, he persecuted the woman who gave birth to the male Child. (14) But the woman was given two wings of a great eagle, that she might fly into the wilderness to her place, where she is nourished for a time and times and half a time, from the presence of the serpent."

The leaves are starting to show

The above passage of scripture, refers to the nation of Israel fleeing the land of Israel, when the Anti-Christ invades that nation. The period of time, that Israel will remain in the wilderness, is exactly the same period of time, that the two witnesses will minister on the earth, i.e. one thousand two hundred and sixty days. When the scripture says that, "they" will feed her there, it is referring to the two witnesses, supernaturally providing for the saints' physical needs. God has done that once before, when Israel was in the wilderness for forty years, and He will do so once again. Both prophets, were used of God to perform miracles of provision when they were on the earth the first time, and both will be used by the Lord in that same manner, once again. You will recall that our Lord Jesus admonished His disciples in Judea, to flee to the mountains, when the Anti-Christ set up his reign in the temple (Matthew 24:16). And so, it will be in the wilderness regions, that the two witnesses will minister to the Lord's saints, during that time. It will be during this time, under the ministries of the two witnesses, that multitudes of Jews, will come to faith in Jesus their Messiah.

Matthew 10:23 "When they persecute you in this city, flee to another. For assuredly, I say to you, you will not have gone through the cities of Israel before the Son of Man comes."

I have stated that Israel, as a nation, will only come to faith in Jesus as their Messiah, when they are in the wilderness, with the Lord's two witnesses. The above passage of scripture confirms this truth, for our Lord Jesus stated, that those who preach the gospel in Israel, would not be able to go through all the towns of Israel, before He returns. Naturally speaking, that is an amazing statement when you think about it, because compared to the rest of the world, the state of Israel, is minuscule. And yet our Lord Jesus said, that the end would not come, before the gospel had been preached throughout the whole world. But when it comes to Israel, our Lord said that His saints would not be able to preach the gospel in every town in that small nation, before He returns. So, how is it possible, that the gospel will be preached throughout the whole world, but not throughout the whole of Israel? The reason is simple. Until the Anti-Christ is manifested, and Israel is forced to flee to the wilderness, she will not be receptive to the gospel, for she will still be observant of the law of Moses. And so, the majority of Jews, will not be saved through the preaching of the gospel in their towns and cities, but rather through the preaching of the Lord's two witnesses, while they are in exile in the wilderness.

Hosea 12:7-9 "A cunning Canaanite! Deceitful scales are in his hand; He loves to oppress. (8) And Ephraim said, 'Surely, I have become rich, I have found wealth for myself; In all my labors They shall find in me no iniquity that is sin.' (9) "But I am the Lord your God, ever since the land of Egypt; I will again make you dwell in tents, As in the days of the appointed feast."

The above passage of scripture highlights three truths for us. The cunning Canaanite in this passage, is referring to the person of the Anti-Christ. Ephraim stating that there is no iniquity in him that is sin, is referring to Israel's spiritual condition at that time, for they will be deceived into thinking that keeping the law of Moses, assures them of salvation. And then we see the Lord telling Israel that He will once again, make them dwell in tents. The appointed feast that our Lord refers to in this passage, is the feast of Tabernacles, for in that feast, Israelis make booths to live in, reminding themselves of the time that they dwelt in tents in the wilderness, when God delivered them from Egypt (Leviticus 23:42-43). In other words, the Holy Spirit is telling us, that just when Israel believes that she is blessed, and living righteously before the Lord, that the Lord will send the Anti-Christ into her midst to oppress, thus driving Israel into the wilderness, to once again, live in tents. It is at that time that the Lord will plead His case with the nation of Israel (Ezekiel 20:35), through His two witnesses. And many will respond, by coming to faith in Jesus their Messiah.

Revelation 14:1-4 "Then I looked, and behold, a Lamb standing on Mount Zion, and with Him one hundred and forty-four thousand, having His Father's name written on their foreheads. ... (4) These are the ones who were not defiled with women, for they are virgins. These are the ones who follow the Lamb wherever He goes. These were redeemed from among men, being first fruits to God and to the Lamb."

Because it falls outside the scope of this teaching, we will not look in any detail, at those the bible refers to, as the "one hundred and forty-four thousand". But I will make a brief mention of them here. The reason for that, is because the one hundred and forty-four thousand, will be among the first Jewish converts, under the ministries of the two witnesses. For notice that the above scripture, refers to them as being first fruits to God and to the Lamb.

The leaves are starting to show

In other words, these Jewish men will be among the first in Israel, to accept Jesus as their Messiah, through the gospel preached by the two witnesses.

Jude 1:9 "Yet Michael the archangel, in contending with the devil, when he disputed about the body of Moses, dared not bring against him a reviling accusation, but said, "The Lord rebuke you!"

So, who are the two witnesses? We know that Elijah himself, is one of the witnesses. And we know that Elijah has never tasted physical death, for God took him into heaven while he was still alive (2 Kings 2:11). So, who is the other witness? As we look at scripture, we clearly see that the second witness is Moses. There are several pointers given to us in scripture, to show us that Moses is the second witness. We know that Moses died physically, because scripture tells us this. But Moses is the only person in the bible, that God instructed the archangel Michael, to bury, and then kept his burial place a secret (Deuteronomy 34:6). We know that Moses body was special. Because, as revealed to us in the above passage of scripture, Satan wanted to have access to it, after Moses death. You will recall that while Moses was alive, that the reflection of God's glory emanating from Moses body was that strong, that he had to wear a veil over his face, when he spoke to the children of Israel (Exodus 34:35). Because Moses body, had been exposed to the glory of God on the mountain, for such a prolonged period (it was eighty days in total), his body could no longer decay, after His spirit left it. That body has still not decayed, and is still reflecting the glory of God, waiting for Moses to enter it once again.

The leaves are starting to show

Luke 9:30-31 "And behold, two men talked with Him, who were Moses and Elijah, (31) who appeared in glory and spoke of His decease which He was about to accomplish at Jerusalem."

And then we have the incident recorded in the above passage of scripture, when our Lord Jesus was transfigured on the mountain. The scripture reveals to us, that the two men who appeared to the Lord on that mountain, were Moses and Elijah. This incident, when they both appeared in glory with our Lord, occurred just before our Lord's death, burial, and resurrection. Of all the old testament prophets, these were the two men chosen by God, to discuss with His Son, that which Jesus was about to accomplish through His death on the cross. Why is that? The answer is revealed in the following passage of scripture.

Zechariah 4:11-14 "Then I answered and said to him, "What are these two olive trees--at the right of the lampstand and at its left?" (12) And I further answered and said to him, "What are these two olive branches that drip into the receptacles of the two gold pipes from which the golden oil drains?" (13) Then he answered me and said, "Do you not know what these are?" And I said, "No, my lord." (14) So, he said, "These are the two anointed ones, who stand beside the Lord of the whole earth."

The above passage of scripture, reveals that there are two anointed ones, that continually stand beside the Lord Jesus, for He is the one, who is the Lord of the whole earth. These are the same two anointed ones, we read about earlier, that appear in the end times, to prophecy and testify of the kingdom of God (Revelation 11:4). It is these two men, Moses and Elijah, that have been chosen by God, to stand in these anointed callings. Both men, had powerful ministries that demonstrated the gift of the working of miracles, when they walked the earth. As we have already seen, the gift of the working of miracles, will be very prominent in their ministries, the second time around.

The Anti-Christ & false prophet revealed

We saw in a previous section, that it is more than likely, that the world's economy will be destroyed by Muslim extremists, who would have acquired nuclear weapons. If that is the case, then what would stop those same terrorists, from using nuclear weapons on the nation of Israel, as well? The answer to that question, is the Anti-Christ himself. It will be very soon after the event of the destruction of the world's economy, that the Anti-Christ will finally be manifested in the earth. We have seen in the section dealing with the ten leaders, that they would align themselves to the Anti-Christ, when he is manifested in the earth. So why do I say, that the Anti-Christ will prevent Muslim extremists from using nuclear weapons on the nation of Israel? The reason he will do that, is because his aim is to proclaim himself as god, in God's temple. And he will be unable to do that, if the city of Jerusalem is uninhabitable, due to radiation fallout from a nuclear explosion.

2 Thessalonians 2:3-12 "Let no one deceive you by any means; for that Day, will not come unless the falling away comes first, and the man of sin is revealed, the son of perdition, (4) who opposes and exalts himself above all that is called God or that is worshiped, so that he sits as God in the temple of God, showing himself that he is God. (5) Do you not remember that when I was still with you I told you these things? (6) And now you know what is restraining, that he may be revealed in his own time. (7) For the mystery of lawlessness is already at work; only He who now restrains will do so until He is taken out of the way. (8) And then the lawless one will be revealed, whom the Lord will consume with the breath of His mouth and destroy with the brightness of His coming. (9) The coming of the lawless one is according to the working of Satan, with all power, signs, and lying wonders, (10) and with all unrighteous deception among those who perish, because they did not receive the love of the truth, that they might be saved. (11) And for this reason, God will send them strong delusion, that they should believe the lie, (12) that they all may be condemned who did not believe the truth but had pleasure in unrighteousness."

This now brings us to the next key event, that must take place, before the end of the age, and that is the revealing of the Anti-Christ. In scripture, the Anti-Christ is given various names. In the above passage, the apostle Paul, calls him the man of sin, the son of perdition, and the lawless one. The apostle John, calls him the Anti-Christ (1 John 2:18), and the beast (Revelation 13:4). It is very amusing to see all the predictions that are made, by various "teachers" of the end times, as to who they say the Anti-Christ is. These predictions range from the latest Pope, to the latest American president, and their predictions always change, when that person either dies, or moves off the world stage. However, the bible reveals to us, a very different person, to any predicted by the many end time teachers that are out there. With regards to the individual, referred to as the Anti-Christ, there are several things that we have already learnt in this teaching, so far. We have seen, that he comes out of the Muslim faith. We have also seen, that he will confront God's two witnesses in the city of Jerusalem, and that He will kill them. This will be an event, that will be seen by the whole world, and the world will rejoice, at his triumph over Moses and Elijah. In the above passage, we see very clearly, that the Anti-Christ will set himself up as god in the earth, and that he will not tolerate the worship of any other than himself, for the scripture says that, he "opposes and exalts himself above all that is called God or that is worshiped, so that he sits as God in the temple of God, showing himself that he is God". Again, we see in this passage, that the temple of God, which we looked at in an earlier section, will be a focal point for him, for he will sit in God's temple, thus showing himself to the world, that he is in fact, god. The above passage of scripture, also reveals to us that he will have supernatural powers, given to him by Satan, and he will be able to perform many miracles, which will have the effect of deceiving all, but the Lord's elect. We also see in this passage, that the Anti-Christ currently exists, and that he existed even at the time that Paul wrote his epistle. For the apostle tells us that he is currently being restrained, and that he will only be revealed, when the one who is restraining him, is taken out of the way. And so, we see that he will be revealed in the earth, only when God ordains that his time has come, for the scripture says, "that he may be revealed in his own time". This passage also tells us plainly, that our Lord Jesus will not return to the earth, until the Anti-Christ has been revealed in the earth, for the scripture says that, "that Day, will not come unless ... the man of sin is revealed". And then finally, we see in this passage, that it is our Lord Jesus Christ, who will be the one who destroys the Anti-Christ when He returns, for the scripture says that, "the Lord will consume (the Anti-Christ) with the breath of His mouth and destroy (the Anti-Christ) with the brightness of His coming". And so, it is also very clear that the Anti-Christ, will be present on the earth, when our Lord Jesus returns to the earth.

Daniel 2:31-39 "You, O king, were watching; and behold, a great image! This great image, whose splendor was excellent, stood before you; and its form was awesome. (32) This image's head was of fine gold, its chest and arms of silver, its belly and thighs of bronze, (33) its legs of iron, its feet partly of iron and partly of clay. ... (36) "This is the dream. Now we will tell the interpretation of it before the king. (37) You, O king, are a king of kings. For the God of heaven has given you a kingdom, power, strength, and glory; (38) and wherever the children of men dwell, or the beasts of the field and the birds of the heaven, He has given them into your hand, and has made you ruler over them all--you are this head of gold. (39) But after you shall arise another kingdom inferior to yours; then another, a third kingdom of bronze, which shall rule over all the earth."

So, what else do we know about this person, called the Anti-Christ? We have also seen earlier in this teaching, that the reign of the Anti-Christ, will not be over the entire globe, but rather over the fourth kingdom, that will be on the earth at that time. For we have seen, that there will be four main kingdoms on the earth, during his time, and that his reign will not extend to the other three kingdoms. Someone will say, but then why does scripture teach us that he will rule over all the earth (Revelation 13:7)? To explain this apparent contradiction, let us look at the statement made by the Holy Spirit through the prophet Daniel, in the above quoted passage of scripture. In this passage, Daniel gave Nebuchadnezzar, the interpretation of a dream that he had received from the Lord. In the interpretation, Daniel tells us that the first kingdom in the dream, was the Babylonian empire. With regards to the first kingdom mentioned by Daniel, God said that He had made Nebuchadnezzar, ruler over all the earth. For He said, "wherever the children of men dwell", He "has made you ruler over them all". And yet, history plainly reveals to us, that although the Babylonian empire under Nebuchadnezzar, was a vast empire, it certainly did not span the entire globe. The extent of that empire, covered the geographic area today, that extended from modern day Iran, to modern day Egypt. The next kingdom referred to by the Holy Spirit in this vision, was the Median empire, which history shows us, was inferior to the Babylonian empire. And then, we come to the third kingdom mentioned, which is referred to as the kingdom of bronze, in this vision. History reveals to us, that this empire was the Persian empire. Again, this empire was extremely vast, in that it included today's geographic areas, extending from modern day Greece, to modern day Egypt, and also reached to the northern parts of modern day India. But even though this empire was extremely vast, it still did not span the entire globe. And yet, God said in this vision, that this empire ruled over all the earth, for the scripture says, "a third kingdom of bronze, which shall rule over all the earth". Now we know that Daniel did not get it wrong, when he gave the interpretation to the vision, because he was led by the inspiration of the Holy Spirit. So why is there this apparent contradiction, with what is recorded in scripture, and historical facts, as we know them to be? The reason that there is an apparent contradiction, is because we in the natural, do not see things as God sees them. For God looks in the realm of the spirit, where the dominions that govern this realm, exist. When the kingdoms that Daniel spoke of, existed on the earth, even though there were other kingdoms on the earth at that time (think of China and South America, for example), none of the other kingdoms existing at that time, could have challenged the power of the kingdoms God spoke of. And as such, they reigned as supreme in the earth. Now bring that concept over into the future, when the Anti-Christ will reign on the earth. The fourth kingdom over which the Anti-Christ will reign at that time, will by far, be the most powerful kingdom in the earth. And so, because the other kingdoms will not be able to challenge his power as such, he will reign as supreme in the earth.

Revelation 17:8 "The beast that you saw was, and is not, and will ascend out of the bottomless pit and go to perdition. And those who dwell on the earth will marvel, whose names are not written in the Book of Life from the foundation of the world, when they see the beast that was, and is not, and yet is."

What else does scripture reveal to us, about this individual? In the book of Revelation, his number is revealed to us, as 666, which the scripture tells us, is the number of a man (Revelation 13:18). And so, we know that the Anti-Christ, is a man. However, although the Anti-Christ is a man, he is not an ordinary man. For in the above passage, the scripture says that, he (referring to the Anti-Christ) "was, and is not, and will ascend out of the bottomless pit". In other words, this passage reveals to us, that he was on the earth once before, and that he is currently being held captive in the bottomless pit, and that he will be released in his time, to come back to the earth. We read earlier, where the apostle Paul, revealed to us in his letter, that the Anti-Christ is currently being restrained. The reason that he is being restrained, is because he is currently being held captive in the bottomless pit. The apostle Paul, also told us that the lawless one will be revealed, once the one who is restraining him, is taken out of the way. In other words, he will only be revealed to the earth, once the angel of the bottomless pit, releases him from captivity.

Genesis 6:1-4 "Now it came to pass, when men began to multiply on the face of the earth, and daughters were born to them, (2) that the sons of God saw the daughters of men, that they were beautiful; and they took wives for themselves of all whom they chose. ... (4) There were giants on the earth in those days, and also afterward, when the sons of God came in to the daughters of men and they bore children to them. Those were the mighty men who were of old, men of renown."

So, how did the Anti-Christ land up in the bottomless pit, in the first place? Although the Anti-Christ is a man, he is also the offspring of an angel. In the above quoted passage of scripture, we see the account of the incident that occurred, when rebel angels left their proper domain, and came to the earth. The "sons of God", referred to in this passage, is in fact, referring to angles, for in this passage, the scripture refers to men, simply as "men", and it refers to women, as "daughters of men". The reason the Holy Spirit does that, is because He wants us to see that the "sons of God", in this passage, is not referring to men, but rather to angels. These angels came to the earth, for the express purpose, of having sexual intercourse with human women. This incident occurred during the time of Noah, before God destroyed the earth with the flood. Notice, that the scripture reveals to us, that children were born to the women that were intimate with these angels. It is also interesting to note, that the male children born, as a result of the union between angels and women, were giants, and mighty men of renown. In other words, they were superior beings, to the rest of mankind on the earth. The one that scripture calls the Anti-Christ, was one of those superior beings, born from these immoral unions. And in fact, the false prophet who will be revealed with the Anti-Christ, at the end of the age, is also one born from those immoral unions.

Jude 1:6-7 "And the angels who did not keep their proper domain, but left their own abode, He has reserved in everlasting chains under darkness for the judgment of the great day; (7) as Sodom and Gomorrah, and the cities around them in a similar manner to these, having given themselves over to sexual immorality and gone after strange flesh, are set forth as an example, suffering the vengeance of eternal fire."

These angels, that came to the earth at that time, were part of Satan's kingdom, but they even rebelled against Satan's authority, in committing this act. For had Satan sanctioned their action, God would have held him to account, when God judged these angels. Satan knows his limits, and will not step out of bounds. For even though he knows the judgement that he is facing, he does not want to incur that judgement, before the time. As revealed in the above passage of scripture, when these rebel angels committed their act, God judged them, by casting them into the bottomless pit, where they are currently being held, awaiting their final judgement. Notice, that the Holy Spirit equates their act, with the sins of Sodom and Gomorrah, in that the people of Sodom and Gomorrah, committed sexual immorality by going after strange flesh, i.e. bestiality. In the same manner, these angels had gone after strange flesh, by having sexual relations with daughters of men. And so, their offspring were part celestial, and part terrestrial, beings. Because of this, when God judged the rebel angels, at the same time, their offspring were also cast into the bottomless pit. For God, will not allow any hybrid species of part angel and part man, to roam free, in His creation. As already mentioned, two of those offspring, are the Anti-Christ and the false prophet. God will release these two, from the bottomless pit, in the end time, to fulfil His purpose. This explains, why the scripture refers to the Anti-Christ in the following manner, as one who, "was, and is not, and will ascend out of the bottomless pit". It is also because these two, are part celestial and part terrestrial beings, that they cannot die, for angels cannot die, as they are immortal beings (Luke 20:36). And so, that is the reason that the book of Revelation reveals to us, that the Anti-Christ and the false prophet, will be cast "alive", into the lake of fire,

The leaves are starting to show

when they are judged (Revelation 19:20). As I have already mentioned, because the Anti-Christ and false prophet are the joint offspring of both angels and men, they will have extraordinary powers, that they will demonstrate on the earth.

Daniel 2:41-43 "Whereas you saw the feet and toes, partly of potter's clay and partly of iron, the kingdom shall be divided; yet the strength of the iron shall be in it, just as you saw the iron mixed with ceramic clay. (42) And as the toes of the feet were partly of iron and partly of clay, so the kingdom shall be partly strong and partly fragile. (43) As you saw iron mixed with ceramic clay, they will mingle with the seed of men; but they will not adhere to one another, just as iron does not mix with clay."

In the above passage of scripture, the prophet Daniel, describes the kingdom of the Anti-Christ that will exist in the earth, when our Lord Jesus returns. I want you to notice the following comment that Daniel made, "they will mingle with the seed of men; but they will not adhere to one another". The "they", that he is referring to in this passage, are the Anti-Christ and the false prophet. Because these two are hybrid beings, and not men, even though they will mingle with men, they will still be separate from them. Because these two, will be superior beings to men, they will view themselves to be gods in the earth, and men will view them, in that same light.

Revelation 13:1-10 "Then I stood on the sand of the sea. And I saw a beast rising up out of the sea, having seven heads and ten horns, and on his horns ten crowns, and on his heads a blasphemous name.

(2) Now the beast which I saw was like a leopard, his feet were like the feet of a bear, and his mouth like the mouth of a lion. The dragon gave him his power, his throne, and great authority. (3) And I saw one of his heads as if it had been mortally wounded, and his deadly wound was healed. And all the world marveled and followed the beast. (4) So, they worshiped the dragon who gave authority to the beast; and they worshiped the beast, saying, "Who is like the beast? Who is able to make war with him?" (5) And he was given a mouth speaking great things and blasphemies, and he was given authority to continue for forty-two months. (6) Then he opened his mouth in blasphemy against God, to blaspheme His name, His tabernacle, and those who dwell in heaven. (7) It was granted to him to make war with the saints and to overcome them. And authority was given him over every tribe, tongue, and nation. (8) All who dwell on the earth will worship him, whose names have not been written in the Book of Life of the Lamb slain from the foundation of the world. (9) If anyone has an ear, let him hear. (10) He who leads into captivity shall go into captivity; he who kills with the sword must be killed with the sword. Here is the patience and the faith of the saints."

The above passage of scripture, reveals some more truths to us, about this person called the Anti-Christ. The "dragon", referred to in this passage, is Satan. And so, we see that the Anti-Christ will receive his power, his authority, and his kingdom, directly from Satan. Although Satan has no authority over the Lord's saints, because we have been delivered from his kingdom, and conveyed into the kingdom of our Lord Jesus (Colossians 1:13), Satan is still the ruler of this world (John 16:11). And as the ruler of this world, he will be able to give the Anti-Christ, his power, his authority, and his kingdom. As part angel himself, the Anti-Christ will have direct contact with Satan (who is also an angel), during his time on the earth. This scripture also reveals to us, that an assassination attempt will be made on the Anti-Christ. The assassination attempt, will be made at the outset of his global reign on the earth, and it will be the event, that will introduce his godlike powers, to those dwelling on the earth. The scripture tells us that he will be mortally wounded, in that attempt. When one is mortally wounded, it means that the wound inflicted upon the person, is the cause of the death of that person. In other words, one who is mortally wounded, always dies as a result of their wound, otherwise the wound would not be mortal. In another passage of scripture, it is revealed to us that a sword will be the instrument that will be used, to inflict this wound (Revelation 13:14). But remember, that the Anti-Christ is part angel, and so he is immortal. The assassination attempt, will be made in full view of the public, when it happens. When the assassination attempt is made on his life, the wound that is inflicted upon him, will be a wound that would always be fatal, if inflicted upon a man. And so, all that witness the assassination attempt, will fully expect the person of the Anti-Christ, to die as a result of the wound inflicted. But instead of his death, the miraculous will occur, for his "mortal" wound, will be miraculously healed, in front of everyone. It is as result of this miracle seen by all, that, "all the world will marvel and follow the beast, and they will worship him, saying, "Who is like the beast? Who is able to make war with him?" From that time onwards, none will challenge his authority in the earth any longer, and he will reign as supreme in the earth. But remember, that his reign will initially only be over the fourth kingdom. Again, we see in this passage, that the period of time, given to the Anti-Christ to reign on the earth, is forty-two months, or three-and-a-half years. It will be during this period, that his reign will begin to extend, over more and more nations in the earth. When the above passage says, that "he will open his mouth in blasphemy against God, to blaspheme His name, His tabernacle, and those who dwell in heaven", it is referring to the fact that the Anti-Christ will from that time, proclaim that he is god in the earth. From the moment that his reign begins on the earth, the Anti-Christ will institute great persecution against the church, for the scripture says that it will be, "granted to him to make war with the saints and to overcome them". This scripture also gives us some insight, into the type of persecution that the saints will suffer during his reign, for the scripture says that, "he who leads into captivity shall go into captivity; he who kills with the sword must be killed with the sword. Here is the patience and the faith of the saints". In other words, the saints can expect to be taken into captivity, and to be killed with the sword. It is interesting to note, that Muslim extremists today, that murder Christian hostages, prefer to do so, by beheading the saints, with a sword. The scripture goes on to tell us, that those who lead the saints into captivity, and kill them with the sword, will experience the same thing themselves, when they are judged, at the end of the age.

Daniel 8:23-25 "And in the latter time of their kingdom, When the transgressors have reached their fullness, A king shall arise, having fierce features, who understands sinister schemes. (24) His power shall be mighty, but not by his own power; He shall destroy fearfully, And shall prosper and thrive; He shall destroy the mighty, and also the holy people. (25) "Through his cunning He shall cause deceit to prosper under his rule; And he shall exalt himself in his heart. He shall destroy many in their prosperity. He shall even rise against the Prince of princes; But he shall be broken without human means."

The above passage of scripture, also describes the person of the Anti-Christ. Notice, that the scripture reveals to us that he understands sinister schemes, and that "through his cunning, he shall cause deceit to prosper under his rule". In other words, not only will the Anti-Christ have miraculous powers, but he will also be a very cunning ruler, able to persuade those around him, to follow after him. It is primarily through this method, that he will rise to power, over the followers of Islam. And it is through this method, that he will engineer a peace treaty, between Israel and the Muslim nations.

Daniel 9:27 "Then he shall confirm a covenant with many for one week; But in the middle of the week He shall bring an end to sacrifice and offering. And on the wing of abominations shall be one who makes desolate, even until the consummation, which is determined, is poured out on the desolate."

It is highly likely that the assassination attempt made on the life of the Anti-Christ, will take place in the city of Jerusalem, and more specifically in the temple. But three-and-a-half years before this event, the Anti-Christ will have already risen to become the leader of the Muslim world. And it will be in that capacity, that he will negotiate a seven-year peace treaty, between the Muslim world and the nation of Israel. The above passage of scripture refers to that event, for it says, "he shall confirm a covenant with many for one week". The scripture goes on to tell us, that the Anti-Christ will bring an end to sacrifice and offering, in the middle of the week. In other words, he will break his treaty with Israel half way through the period of that treaty, and in doing so, he will bring an end to Israel's temple worship. As we will see later in this teaching, the reason that he will be able to put a stop to Israel's temple worship, is because his armies will invade Israel at that time.

Revelation 11:7-13 "When they finish their testimony, the beast that ascends out of the bottomless pit will make war against them, overcome them, and kill them. (8) And their dead bodies will lie in the street of the great city which spiritually is called Sodom and Egypt, where also our Lord was crucified. (9) Then those from the peoples, tribes, tongues, and nations will see their dead bodies three-and-a-half days, and not allow their dead bodies to be put into graves. (10) And those who dwell on the earth will rejoice over them, make merry, and send gifts to one another, because these two prophets tormented those who dwell on the earth. (11) Now after the three-and-a-half days the breath of life from God entered them, and they stood on their feet, and great fear fell on those who saw them. (12) And they heard a loud voice from heaven saying to them, "Come up here." And they ascended to heaven in a cloud, and their enemies saw them. (13) In the same hour there was a great earthquake, and a tenth of the city fell. In the earthquake seven

The leaves are starting to show

thousand people were killed, and the rest were afraid and gave glory to the God of heaven."

We have already looked at the above passage of scripture, when we discussed the Lord's two witnesses, but we will relook at it in this section, because it involves the person of the Anti-Christ. The Anti-Christ will set up his reign, from the temple in Jerusalem. Towards the end of his reign, the two witnesses will confront him in the city of Jerusalem, and scripture reveals to us, that the Anti-Christ will kill them. The reason that the Anti-Christ will overcome the two prophets of the Lord, is because he is part angel, and in this life, angels are greater in power and might, than men are (2 Peter 2:11). The Anti-Christ will not allow their bodies to be buried, but will rather display their dead bodies to the earth. And the earth will rejoice in the fact, that their champion has finally slain the prophets of the Lord. But the scripture also reveals to us that their joy will be short lived, for God will raise His two prophets from the dead, in full view of everyone. When we look at the false prophet in the following passage of scripture, we will see that the false prophet always reminds the earth, about the Anti-Christ's recovery from his deadly wound, but never reminds the earth about how the beast killed the two witnesses, even though the whole world will witness that event. The reason for that, is because this incident will only take place at the end of the Anti-Christ's reign. And also, if the Anti-Christ were to kill the two witnesses at the start of his reign, then according to this passage of scripture, he would have a problem trying to convince the rest of the world to follow him, because the world would have seen God raise His two prophets, from the dead. So, the question arises, as to why the Anti-Christ will wait three-and-a-half years before manifesting himself to the world, as god in the earth? The answer to that question, lies in the person of the false prophet. For as we will see in scripture, the Anti-Christ will not manifest his supernatural powers, until the false prophet is manifested in the earth.

Revelation 13:11-18 "Then I saw another beast coming up out of the earth, and he had two horns like a lamb and spoke like a dragon. (12) And he exercises all the authority of the first beast in his presence, and causes the earth and those who dwell in it to worship the first beast, whose deadly wound was healed. (13) He performs great signs, so that he even makes fire come down from heaven on the earth in the sight of men. (14) And he deceives those who dwell on the earth--by those signs which he was granted to do in the sight of the beast, telling those who dwell on the earth to make an image to the beast who was wounded by the sword and lived. (15) He was granted power to give breath to the image of the beast, that the image of the beast should both speak and cause as many as would not worship the image of the beast to be killed. (16) He causes all, both small and great, rich and poor, free and slave, to receive a mark on their right hand or on their foreheads, (17) and that no one may buy or sell except one who has the mark or the name of the beast, or the number of his name. (18) Here is wisdom. Let him who has understanding calculate the number of the beast, for it is the number of a man: His number is 666."

And so, we come to the person called the false prophet (Revelation 16:13). The above passage of scripture, gives us some insight into who this individual is, and what his role will be in the earth, in the last days. It is significant, that the beast called the false prophet, is only manifested in the earth, after the Anti-Christ is manifested. What is equally significant, is that it seems as if God prohibits the Anti-Christ from displaying any supernatural powers, until the false prophet is revealed in the earth. For we see no evidence, of any of the Anti-Christ's supernatural powers displayed, until the false prophet is revealed. And in fact, scripture only describes the false prophet as the one who performs miraculous signs, even though the scripture attributes the power, as coming from the Anti-Christ. And so, this answers the question, as to why the Anti-Christ only displays himself as god in the earth, halfway through his reign of seven years. He does that, because he has to wait for the false prophet to be revealed, before he is able to display his supernatural power. We have already seen that the false prophet is also a hybrid being, in that he is part angel and part man. But although the false prophet will also be a superior being in the earth, he will not have the same level of supernatural power, as the Anti-Christ, for don't forget, that we have seen that Satan will give his power, to the Anti-Christ. The reason that I say that the false prophet will not be as powerful as the Anti-Christ, is because the scripture tells us that he is only able to perform certain miracles, when in the presence of the Anti-Christ. For the scripture says that, "he deceives those who dwell on the earth, by those signs which he was granted to do, in the sight of the beast". One of the signs that he will be able to perform, is that he will make fire come down from heaven on the earth, in the sight of men. It is also the false prophet, that will be instrumental, in extending the reach of the fourth kingdom in the earth, for the scripture says that he is the one, who will cause the earth and those who dwell in it, to worship the Anti-Christ. In other words, he will go through the earth, to persuade more and more nations in the earth, to become a part of the fourth kingdom. One of the ways that the false prophet will accomplish this, is that he will instruct those who dwell on the earth, to make an image to the beast, and he will be granted power to give breath to the image of the beast, so that the image of the beast will be able to speak, and cause as many as refuse to worship the image of the beast, to be killed. It is interesting to note, that in persuading many on the earth to worship the beast, that the false prophet will very often, remind them of the incident of the beast being healed from his deadly wound. Again, this gives us a strong indication, that many people around the world, would have witnessed the assassination attempt, made on the life of the Anti-Christ. And then finally, we also see in this passage, that it is the false prophet, that will introduce the mark of the beast, into the earth. That mark, will be placed on either the right hand, or on the foreheads, of those who choose to follow the beast, and no one will be allowed to buy or sell, except those who have the mark or the name of the beast, or the number of his name, which is 666. We have already seen, that all in the fourth kingdom will gladly receive the mark of the beast, but obviously, for the saints dwelling in nations that decide to join the fourth kingdom during that time, it will be another form of persecution that will be used against them. So, how do the Anti-Christ and the false prophet, tie in with the religion of Islam? For we have seen throughout this teaching so far, that Islam, features very strongly in end time events. And therefore, because Islam features so strongly in end time events, it is essential that these two characters, should also tie in with the religion of Islam.

And that is exactly the case. For the religion of Islam, also has two end time characters, that Muslims are waiting for, to be revealed in the earth. The first one is called al-Mahdi, and the second is called Isa. The Mahdi (literally "guided one"), is an eschatological redeemer of Islam, who will appear and will rule for five, seven, nine, or nineteen years (according to differing interpretations) before the Day of Judgement (*yawm al-qiyamah*, literally, *the Day of Resurrection*), and will violently rid the world of evil. There is no reference to the Mahdi in the Quran, only in the ahadith (the reports and traditions of Muhammad's teachings collected after his death). In most traditions, Mahdi will arrive with Isa to defeat Masih ad-Dajjal (literally, the "false Messiah"). Although the concept of a Mahdi is not an essential doctrine in Sunni Islam, he is popular among both Sunni and Shi'a Muslims. Both agree that he will rule over the Muslims and establish justice[13]. Clearly the person called the Mahdi, in Islam, is the person revealed as the Anti-Christ, in scripture. For there are several similarities, as revealed in scripture. From scripture, we understand that the Anti-Christ will rule over the fourth kingdom for a total of seven years, and extend his rule in the second half of those seven years, to encompass the rest of the world, before God's judgement takes place in the earth. In Islam, one of the Muslim expectations is that the Mahdi will rule for seven years, before the day of judgement. Scripture states that the Anti-Christ will make war with the Lord's saints, and overcome them, in other words, he will kill them. In Islam, the Muslim belief is that the Mahdi will violently rid the world of evil. Scripture states that the Anti-Christ will kill the Lord's two prophets. In Islam, the Muslim belief is that the Mahdi will defeat or kill, what they call, the false Messiah. But the tie in with scripture goes even further than that, for as the person of the Mahdi is revealed as the Anti-Christ, so the person of the false prophet, is clearly revealed as the prophet, Islam calls, Isa. In Islam, Isa, is the name of the person they call the prophet, Jesus.

Both Sunni and Shi'a Muslims agree that al-Mahdi will arrive first, and after him, Isa. Isa will proclaim al-Mahdi as the Islamic community leader. A war will be fought—the Dajjal against al-Mahdi and Isa. This war will mark the approach of the coming of the Last Day. After Isa slays al-Dajjal at the Gate of Lod, he will bear witness and reveal that Islam is indeed the true and last word from God to humanity as Yusuf Ali's translation reads: "And there is none of the People of the Book but must believe in him before his death; and on the Day of Judgment he will be a witness against them" (Quran 4:159)[14]. As we have already seen in scripture, the false prophet is only manifested in the earth, after the Anti-Christ. And Islam believes, that their prophet, Isa, will arrive on the earth after the Mahdi. The scripture reveals to us, that the false prophet will be the one who is instrumental, in persuading the world to follow the Anti-Christ. And Islam believes, that Isa will proclaim al-Mahdi as the Islamic community leader. Although scripture does not explicitly state, that the false prophet will be with the Anti-Christ, when he kills Elijah and Moses, it would be highly unlikely that the false prophet will not be standing alongside his superior, when that confrontation takes place. For you will recall that we have stated, that it seems as if it is the false prophet, that actually demonstrates the power of the Anti-Christ, while in his presence. And Islam believes, that both Isa and the Mahdi will defeat or kill the "false Messiah". And so, those who the Muslims believe to be the false "Messiah", we know to be, the Lord's two prophets. Scripture teaches us, that the Anti-Christ will kill the two witnesses, in the city of Jerusalem. And Islam believes, that their Mahdi will kill the "false Messiah", in the city of Lod in Israel, which is approximately forty-five kilometres from Jerusalem. Although the Muslims get the city wrong, they get the nation right, for it is in Israel, that this confrontation will take place. And so, we see that scripture clearly spoke about the two central figures of Islam, as relating to the end times, four hundred years before the religion of Islam, was even introduced into the earth. This is just further evidence, that Islam is the fourth kingdom, and that it is from the religion of Islam, that the Anti-Christ and the false prophet will emerge.

Revelation 19:19-21 "And I saw the beast, the kings of the earth, and their armies, gathered together to make war against Him who sat on the horse and against His army. (20) Then the beast was captured, and with him the false prophet who worked signs in his presence, by which he deceived those who received the mark of the beast and those who worshiped his image. These two were cast alive into the lake of fire burning with brimstone. (21) And the rest were killed with the sword which proceeded from the mouth of Him who sat on the horse. And all the birds were filled with their flesh."

At the end of the reign of the Anti-Christ, the church will be caught away from the earth, and the wrath of God will be poured out on the earth. God's wrath will be poured out on the earth, for a period of just under three years. At the end of that time, our Lord Jesus will return to the earth with His saints, to reign on the earth. As revealed in the above passage of scripture, it is at our

Lord's return, that the battle of Armageddon will take place, and it is at that time that the Anti-Christ and the false prophet, will be cast alive into the lake of fire and brimstone. In fact, they will be the first two individuals to be cast into that lake, even before Satan. But notice also, that they will be cast into the lake, "alive". The reason for that, as we have already seen, is because they are part angel, and therefore immortal.

Chapter 4

Summer is at the door

Jewish believers flee Israel

Luke 21:5-24 "Then, as some spoke of the temple, how it was adorned with beautiful stones and donations, He said, (6) "These things which you see--the days will come in which not one stone shall be left upon another that shall not be thrown down." (7) So, they asked Him, saying, "Teacher, but when will these things be? And what sign will there be when these things are about to take place?" (8) And He said: ... (20) "But when you see Jerusalem surrounded by armies, then know that its desolation is near. (21) Then let those who are in Judea flee to the mountains, let those who are in the midst of her depart, and let not those who are in the country enter her. (22) For these are the days of vengeance, that all things which are written may be fulfilled. (23) But woe to those who are pregnant and to those who are nursing babies in those days! For there will be great distress in the land and wrath upon this people. (24) And they will fall by the edge of the sword, and be led away captive into all nations. And Jerusalem will be trampled by Gentiles until the times of the Gentiles are fulfilled."

This brings us to the next key event that must take place, before our Lord Jesus returns to the earth. And that is the event of the Jewish believers, fleeing Israel. As we have already seen in a previous section, there is coming a time when the Anti-Christ, will be manifested in the city of Jerusalem. So just how will this happen? In the gospels, our Lord Jesus spoke of two separate occasions, where He warned His disciples to flee Judea. The first occasion, was when the Roman empire destroyed the temple and the city of Jerusalem, in the year 70 AD. That account was recorded for us in Luke's gospel, which I have quoted above. As we can see, in Luke's gospel account, our Lord was speaking to all His disciples, while they were standing in the temple, and He was answering their question, regarding what would happen to the temple, that they were standing in. In His teaching, our Lord also spoke of events that would occur leading up to the end of the age, but in the section that I have quoted, our Lord was specifically addressing, what would happen to the temple, the city of Jerusalem, and Judea, that existed at that time. And so, in answer to their question, our Lord instructed His disciples to flee Judea, when they saw the following sign, i.e. the sign of the city of Jerusalem, being surrounded by armies. Jesus specifically warned the disciples, living in Jerusalem at that time, to leave the city. And He instructed the disciples living outside the city, not to enter the city. This sign came to pass, in the year 66 AD. In that year, Rome sent an army, to put down the Jewish rebellion that had erupted in Judea. That army, came to the outer walls of the city of Jerusalem, but could not penetrate it. The commander of that Roman army then withdrew, leaving the city intact[15]. The Jewish believers, living in Jerusalem at that time, recognised the sign given to them by our Lord, and they then left the city. They fled to a town called Pella, on the east side of the river Jordan[16]. Meanwhile the Jewish rebellion against Rome continued, and four years later, the Roman armies returned to Jerusalem. It was during the feast of Passover, when multitudes of Jews had come to Jerusalem to celebrate the feast, that the Roman armies once again, surrounded the city. This time was different however, because this time the Romans took the city, and in the process, destroyed both the city, and the temple. Historical accounts of that event, record that hundreds of thousands of Jews, that were trapped in the city, were killed, and nearly one hundred thousand were taken into slavery[17]. But the Jewish believers were not affected, because they had heeded the Lord's warning, and left the city the first time that the city was surrounded by armies. Had they waited, until the second time the city was surrounded by the Roman armies, they would not have been able to escape. And they would have been killed, along with all the unbelieving Jews, that were slaughtered at that time.

Mark 13:1-20 "Then as He went out of the temple, one of His disciples said to Him, "Teacher, see what manner of stones and what buildings are here!" (2) And Jesus answered and said to him, "Do you see these great buildings? Not one stone shall be left upon another, that shall not be thrown down." (3) Now as He sat on the Mount of Olives opposite the temple, Peter, James, John, and Andrew asked Him privately, (4) "Tell us, when will these things be? And what will be the sign when all these things will be fulfilled?" (5) And Jesus, answering them, began to say: ... (14) "So when you see the 'Abomination of desolation,' spoken of by Daniel the prophet, standing where it ought not" (let the reader understand), "then let those who are in Judea flee to the mountains. (15) Let him who is on the housetop not go down into the house, nor enter to take anything out of his house. (16) And let him who is in the field not go back to get his clothes. (17) But woe to those who are pregnant and to those who are nursing babies in those days! (18) And pray that your flight may not be in winter. (19) For in those days there will be tribulation, such as has not been since the beginning of the creation which God created until this time, nor ever shall be. (20) And unless the Lord had shortened those days, no flesh would be saved; but for the elect's sake, whom He chose, He shortened the days."

This brings us to the second occasion, where our Lord warned those living in Judea, to flee to the mountains. This second occasion refers to the future event, still to take place. That account has been recorded for us in Mark's gospel, which I have quoted above. Matthew's gospel records this same account for us, almost word for word (Matthew 24). In both Mark and Matthew's gospel accounts, our Lord Jesus was speaking privately to Peter, James, John and Andrew, while they were seated on the mount of Olives. And so, in this account, our Lord elaborated on what He had already taught all the disciples, in the temple, but with one major difference. The difference was, that He now spoke of the end time event, and not the event that would occur in the year 70 AD. And so, we see that on the second occasion, where our Lord warns His disciples living in Judea, to flee to the mountains, our Lord instructions are different this time. The reason for that, is because the scenario on the second occasion, will be completely different. The sign given to the saints, for the end time event, will be the sign of the Anti-Christ himself, physically standing in the temple. For that is what our Lord is referring to, when He says, "So when you see the 'Abomination of desolation,' spoken of by Daniel the prophet, standing where it ought not". And so, it is when they see that sign, that our Lord tells His saints to flee Judea, not before. You will recall, that on the first occasion that our Lord told His saints to flee Judea, that in effect, He gave them their warning sign, four years before disaster overtook those dwelling in Jerusalem. On the second occasion however, the saints will not be afforded the same timeframe of warning, to flee Judea. In fact, the time frame, from the time that the saints see the sign, and disaster striking, will be extremely short. Because, notice on this occasion, that our Lord tells His saints, to not even go into their homes to pack. He tells them to drop whatever they are doing, and leave. Our Lord would not give His saints their warning, when it will be too late to do anything about it. And so, when the saints see the sign of the Anti-Christ standing in the temple, they will have time to flee Judea, but they must do so immediately. Because all Jews would have returned to Israel by that time, there will be approximately sixteen million Jews living in Israel, when this event occurs. However, because the two witnesses would not yet have been manifested to Israel, the vast majority of the nation, will still be unbelievers. And so, because most Jews at that time will be unbelievers, they will not recognise the sign that the Lord has given to His saints, and so there will not be an exodus of sixteen million Jews, fleeing to the mountains. Because most in Israel at that time, will be Jews who observe the Sabbath, our Lord tells His saints to pray that their flight will not be on a Sabbath (Matthew 24:20). The reason for that, is because most of Israel will shut down for the Sabbath, and it will therefore be that much more difficult to travel. Nevertheless, those who are saved, will recognise the sign given to them by our Lord Jesus, and will flee to the mountains.

Daniel 8:23-25 "And in the latter time of their kingdom, When the transgressors have reached their fullness, A king shall arise, having fierce features, who understands sinister schemes. (24) His power shall be mighty, but not by his own power; He shall destroy fearfully, and shall prosper and thrive; He shall destroy the mighty, and also the holy people. (25) "Through his cunning, He shall cause deceit to prosper under his rule; And he shall exalt himself in his heart. He shall destroy many in their prosperity. He shall even rise against the Prince of princes; But he shall be broken without human means."

Scripture does not give us any detail, as to just how it will come about, that the Anti-Christ will stand in the temple. But it would be safe to say, that this will not happen, as a result of the armies of the Anti-Christ invading Israel. For if we refer back to the warning that our Lord has given His saints, it is only after they see the Anti-Christ standing in the temple, that they are instructed to flee. If the Anti-Christ, were to gain access to the temple by means of an invading army, then by the time his army had taken control of the temple area, it would be too late for the saints in Jerusalem to flee, for they would already be under the control of those invading armies. But rather, it seems as if it will be, by means of cunning and deceit, that the Anti-Christ will gain access to the temple, for the above passage of scripture describes the Anti-Christ, as just such a person.

Summer is at the door

Daniel 9:27 "Then he shall confirm a covenant with many for one week; But in the middle of the week he shall bring an end to sacrifice and offering. And on the wing of abominations shall be one who makes desolate, even until the consummation, which is determined, is poured out on the desolate."

As we have already seen, the scriptures refer to the Anti-Christ as one who is cunning, and who understands sinister schemes. Before the event of the Anti-Christ standing in the temple, he would have already risen as the leader of the fourth kingdom. As the leader of that kingdom, he will negotiate a peace treaty with Israel and the Muslim nations, that surround her. Scripture reveals to us in the book of Daniel quoted above, that this covenant or peace treaty, will be a seven-year peace treaty. The above scripture, informs us that he will break that treaty in the middle of that seven-year period, by bringing an end to sacrifice and offering. It is entirely possible, that the assassination attempt made on the life of the Anti-Christ, will take place on this occasion, when the he stands in the temple. You will recall that when this incident takes place, that the world will see his supernatural powers being displayed. Nevertheless, this event will take Israel by surprise, and will result in the armies of the Anti-Christ invading and conquering Israel as a nation.

Zechariah 14:1-4 "Behold, the day of the Lord is coming, and your spoil will be divided in your midst. (2) For I will gather all the nations to battle against Jerusalem; The city shall be taken, the houses rifled, And the women ravished. Half of the city shall go into captivity, But the remnant of the people shall not be cut off from the city. (3) Then the Lord will go forth and fight against those nations, As He fights in the day of battle. (4) And in that day His feet will stand on the Mount of Olives, which faces Jerusalem on the east. And the Mount of Olives shall be split in two, from east to west, making a very large valley; Half of the mountain shall move toward the north and half of it toward the south."

There will be a war, in which the armies of the Anti-Christ, will defeat the Israeli army. The above passage of scripture, gives us a vivid account of what will take place in the city of Jerusalem, during that war. Obviously, what will happen in Jerusalem, will happen throughout Israel during that time. When the scripture says that the "remnant of the people", will not be cut off from the city, it is referring to the Lord's saints, for they are the remnant (Romans 11:5). The reason that they will not be cut off from the city, is because they would have already left the city, and so will not experience the tragedy that will befall the rest of the Jews in the city. The very next verse of scripture in this passage, describes the battle of Armageddon that will take place when our Lord Jesus returns, to take vengeance on the people of the fourth kingdom, that invaded the nation of Israel.

Psalms 79:1-13 "O God, the nations have come into Your inheritance; Your holy temple they have defiled; They have laid Jerusalem in heaps. (2) The dead bodies of Your servants-- They have given as food for the birds of the heavens, The flesh of Your saints to the beasts of the earth. (3) Their blood they have shed like water all around Jerusalem, and there was no one to bury them. (4) We have become a reproach to our neighbors, A scorn and derision to those who are around us. (5) How long, Lord? Will You be angry forever? Will Your jealousy burn like fire? (6) Pour out Your wrath on the nations that do not know You, and on the kingdoms, that do not call on Your name. (7) For they have devoured Jacob, And laid waste his dwelling place. (8) Oh, do not remember former iniquities against us! Let Your tender mercies come speedily to meet us, for we have been brought very low. (9) Help us, O God of our salvation, For the glory of Your name; And deliver us, and provide atonement for our sins, For Your name's sake! (10) Why should the nations say, "Where is their God?" Let there be known among the nations in our sight the avenging of the blood of Your servants which has been shed. (11) Let the groaning of the prisoner come before You; According to the greatness of Your power preserve those who are appointed to die; (12) And return to our neighbors sevenfold into their bosom Their reproach with which they have reproached You, O Lord. (13) So, we, Your people and sheep of Your pasture, will give You thanks forever; We will show forth Your praise to all generations."

Many have thought, that the above quoted passage of scripture, refers to the destruction of the first temple that took place, when the Jews were taken captive to Babylon, in the year 587 BC. And some have thought, that this passage refers to the destruction of the second temple that took place, when the Jews were taken captive by Rome, in the year 70 AD. But neither of those assumptions are correct, for this passage actually refers to the defiling of the third temple that will take place, when the Anti-Christ invades Israel. There are two main keys in this passage, that reveal to us, that this event is still to take place. Firstly, although the scripture says that these invading armies will lay Jerusalem in heaps, it does not say that the temple is destroyed, only defiled. On both occasions however, in 587 BC and 70 AD, those temples were completely destroyed. Secondly, this passage refers to the Lord returning to Israel's neighbors, sevenfold into their bosom their reproach, with which they have reproached the Lord. On both occasions, in 587 BC and 70 AD, Israel was not invaded by her neighbors, but rather by foreign powers, from distant lands. It is only when the Anti-Christ invades the nation of Israel, that she will be invaded by her Muslim neighbors.

Psalms 83:1-13 "Do not keep silent, O God! Do not hold Your peace, and do not be still, O God! (2) For behold, Your enemies make a tumult; And those who hate You have lifted up their head. (3) They have taken crafty counsel against Your people, and consulted together against Your sheltered ones. (4) They have said, "Come, and let us cut them off from being a nation, That the name of Israel may be remembered no more." (5) For they have consulted together with one consent; They form a confederacy against You: (6) The tents of Edom and the Ishmaelites; Moab and the Hagrites; (7) Gebal, Ammon, and Amalek; Philistia with the inhabitants of Tyre; (8) Assyria also has joined with them; They have helped the children of Lot. ... (13) O my God, make them like the whirling dust, Like the chaff before the wind!"

Summer is at the door

The Holy Spirit revealed to us in the Psalms, the ten nations that will conspire to destroy the nation of Israel in the last days. It is these nations that make up the ten kings, referred to in Daniels vision. It is these ten nations that will align themselves to the Anti-Christ when he is revealed. Each of the nations mentioned in the Psalms, equate to modern nations, that form part of Islam today.

Revelation 12:7-17 "And war broke out in heaven: Michael and his angels fought with the dragon; and the dragon and his angels fought, (8) but they did not prevail, nor was a place found for them in heaven any longer. (9) So, the great dragon was cast out, that serpent of old, called the Devil and Satan, who deceives the whole world; he was cast to the earth, and his angels were cast out with him. (10) Then I heard a loud voice saying in heaven, "Now salvation, and strength, and the kingdom of our God, and the power of His Christ have come, for the accuser of our brethren, who accused them before our God day and night, has been cast down. (11) And they overcame him by the blood of the Lamb and by the word of their testimony, and they did not love their lives to the death. (12) Therefore rejoice, O heavens, and you who dwell in them! Woe to the inhabitants of the earth and the sea! For the devil has come down to you, having great wrath, because he knows that he has a short time." (13) Now when the dragon saw that he had been cast to the earth, he persecuted the woman who gave birth to the male Child. (14) But the woman was given two wings of a great eagle, that she might fly into the wilderness to her place, where she is nourished for a time and times and half a time, from the presence of the serpent. (15) So, the serpent spewed water out of his mouth like a flood after the woman, that he might cause her to be carried away by the flood. (16) But the earth helped the woman, and the earth opened its mouth and swallowed up the flood which the dragon had spewed out of his mouth. (17) And the dragon was enraged with the woman, and he went to make war with the rest of her offspring, who keep the commandments of God and have the testimony of Jesus Christ."

We must never forget, that the end time events that we see unfold on the earth, all have their origin, in the spirit realm. The above passage of scripture, reveals some of the spiritual events, that will take place in the end days, which will then obviously impact on events that will take place in this realm. There is coming a time, when all-out war will break out in heaven, for God will release the Archangel Michael and his angels, to invade the realm of heaven, where Satan and his angels currently reside. As we will see, that time has not yet come. The scripture reveals to us, that Michael and his angels will prevail against Satan and his angels, and that they will finally, be cast out of heaven. Someone will say, but I thought that Jesus said, that He already saw Satan cast out of heaven like lightning (Luke 10:18). Scripture reveals to us, that there is more than one heaven, for the apostle Paul mentioned, that on one occasion, that the Lord had taken him up to the third heaven (2 Corinthians 12:2). And so, the incident that our Lord referred to, was the incident when Satan had entered into the heaven where God's throne is, and tried to overthrow God from His throne, and it was from that heaven, that Satan was cast out, like lightning. The angels that fall under Satan's control, have always dwelt in a heavenly realm which is located just above the earth, for the scripture teaches us that Satan's angels, are "spiritual hosts of wickedness in the heavenly places" (Ephesians 6:12). When Satan was cast out of the heaven where God's throne is, he was cast to the heavenly realm, where he and his angels currently reside. And so, we see that when Michael and his angels prevail against Satan, that Satan and his angels will be cast out of their heavenly realm, to the earth. We need to understand the impact that this event will have on the earth, for ever since God created Satan and his angels, they have always dwelt in their heavenly realm, and now the reality of their impending eternal judgement, will strike home, and they will desperately want to destroy any, who are part of God's kingdom. We see in this passage, that the first people, that Satan will try to destroy, are the children of Israel. But he will be unsuccessful in that attempt, because as we have already discussed in an earlier section, those saints will flee to the wilderness. And then we see, that Satan will go after the rest of the Lord's saints, dwelling on the earth at that time. Obviously, Satan will do all of this, through the persons of the Anti-Christ and the false prophet, for in the very next chapter in the book of Revelation, we see the description, of both the Anti-Christ and the false prophet, being made manifest in the earth (Revelation chapter 13). And so, we see that the event of Satan and his angels being cast to the earth, will be the catalyst for the Anti-Christ and the false prophet, being made manifest in the earth. That is why the scripture tells us, that Satan knows that he has a short time, for he knows that God will only allow the Anti-Christ to rule, for forty-two months.

The great tribulation

Summer is at the door

Jeremiah 30:4-7 "Now these are the words that the Lord spoke concerning Israel and Judah. (5) "For thus says the Lord: 'We have heard a voice of trembling, Of fear, and not of peace. (6) Ask now, and see, whether a man is ever in labor with child? So why do I see every man with his hands on his loins like a woman in labor, and all faces turned pale? (7) Alas! For that day is great, so that none is like it; And it is the time of Jacob's trouble, but he shall be saved out of it."

Our Lord Jesus, has taught us about the great tribulation, that would take place in the last days. As we have seen in the previous section, that persecution will begin in the nation of Israel, and from there, it will spread to the rest of the world. Because the Anti-Christ will reign from the city of Jerusalem, Israel will bear the brunt of the persecution, instituted by the Anti-Christ. The above passage of scripture, gives us an account of what that time of persecution will be like, and it deals specifically with the nation of Israel, because the Holy Spirit says that, "these are the words that the Lord spoke concerning Israel and Judah". The scripture calls it, "the time of Jacob's trouble", and that this time of trouble will be great, "so that none is like it". Think about that statement for a moment. Both the Jews, and the world today, think that the persecution suffered by the Jews, during the holocaust, was the worst persecution in their history. And yet, the scripture tells us that there is coming a time, when the Jews will suffer an even greater persecution, than the holocaust. The Jews today, have vowed that the holocaust will never happen again, but sadly, the bible teaches us differently. But I also want you to notice, that regarding Jacob's day of trouble, that our Lord says, "but he shall be saved out of it". The reason that the Holy Spirit says, that Israel will be saved out of it, is because it will be during this period of intense persecution, that the nation of Israel, will turn to Jesus their Messiah.

Matthew 24:21-27 "For then there will be great tribulation, such as has not been since the beginning of the world until this time, no, nor ever shall be. (22) And unless those days were shortened, no flesh would be saved; but for the elect's sake those days will be shortened. (23) "Then if anyone says to you, 'Look, here is the Christ!' or 'There!' do not believe it. (24) For false christs and false prophets will rise and show great signs and wonders to deceive, if possible, even the elect. (25) See, I have told you beforehand. (26) "Therefore, if they say to you, 'Look, He is in the desert!' do not go out; or 'Look, He is in the inner rooms!' do not believe it. (27) For as the lightning comes from the east and flashes to the west, so also will the coming of the Son of Man be."

The church is not appointed to wrath (1 Thessalonians 5:9), but she is appointed to tribulation (1 Thessalonians 3:3). And so, the church will not experience the wrath of God that is to be poured out on the earth, as is recorded in the book of Revelation. Scripture teaches us, that before God's wrath is poured out on the earth, that the church will be caught away from the earth, in the first resurrection. However, the last key event that will take place on the earth, before the first resurrection, is the event that our Lord called, the "great tribulation". In the above passage of scripture, our Lord tells us, that the level of tribulation experienced during that time, will be greater than any experienced on the earth before. If you think of past trials that have taken place on the earth, such as the Jewish holocaust for example, our Lord's statement is very sobering indeed. The tribulation period that our Lord was referring to, is the period when the Anti-Christ, will reign in the earth. Therefore, our heavenly Father has shortened the days of the reign of the Anti-Christ. Because if He hadn't, then no flesh would be saved in that time. When our Lord tells us, that no flesh would be saved unless those days had been shortened, He is referring to saints still being found alive on the earth. For during that time, as revealed to us in the book of Revelation, there will be multitudes of the Lord's saints, who will be martyred on the earth (Revelation 15:2). Because this will be a severe time of trial for the saints, they will be tempted to look at the many false christs and false prophets, that will rise up at that time. The temptations will be real, because the false christs and false prophets will show great signs and wonders to deceive, if possible, even the elect.

Luke 17:22-33 "Then He said to the disciples, "The days will come when you will desire to see one of the days of the Son of Man, and you will not see it. (23) And they will say to you, 'Look here!' or 'Look there!' Do not go after them or follow them. (24) For as the lightning that flashes out of one part under heaven shines to the other part under heaven, so also the Son of Man will be in His day. (25) But first He must suffer many things and be rejected by this generation. (26) And as it was in the days of Noah, so it will be also in the days of the Son of Man: (27) They ate, they drank, they married wives, they were given in marriage, until the day that Noah entered the ark, and the flood came and destroyed them all. (28) Likewise, as it was also in the days of Lot: They ate, they drank, they bought, they sold, they planted, they built; (29) but on the day that Lot went out of Sodom it rained fire and brimstone from heaven and destroyed them all. (30) Even so will it be in the day when the Son of Man is revealed. (31) "In that day, he who is on the housetop, and his goods are in the house, let him not come down to take them away. And likewise, the one who is in the field, let him not turn back. (32) Remember Lot's wife. (33) Whoever seeks to save his life will lose it, and whoever loses his life will preserve it."

Scripture clearly reveals to us that the Anti-Christ will reign over the earth for forty-two months. As revealed to us by the Lord, in the gospel of Luke quoted above, the message of the gospel will no longer be openly preached in the earth, at that time. But remember that the Anti-Christ will only reign over the fourth kingdom. And so initially, the persecution of the saints, will only impact the saints living in the nations, that form part of the fourth kingdom. But as we have already seen, scripture reveals to us that the false prophet, that will work with the Anti-Christ, will be the main instigator, in bringing more and more nations into the fold of Islam, and worship of the Anti-Christ. As the false prophet goes into the earth, to convince more and more nations to turn to Islam, and following the beast, so the persecution against the Lord's saints, living in those nations, will increase. As we draw closer to the end time, Christians should be aware of any growing influence of Islam, in the nations in which they reside. For all nations, that have a significant portion of their population which are Muslim, will very quickly fall under the influence of the Anti-Christ, during his reign. It is in these nations, and the nation of Israel, that all Jewish and Gentile believers, will suffer extreme persecution.

Revelation 13:16-17 "He causes all, both small and great, rich and poor, free and slave, to receive a mark on their right hand or on their foreheads, (17) and that no one may buy or sell except one who has the mark or the name of the beast, or the number of his name."

As we have already seen earlier, the saints will also suffer economic persecution during this time, because as mentioned in the above passage of scripture, all who refuse to receive the mark of the beast, will be forbidden from buying or selling, anything. And so, we see that as the false prophet persuades more and more nations, to bow their knee to the reign of the Anti-Christ, that one of the first things that he will introduce into those nations, is receiving the mark of the beast, thus making it impossible for the saints, to hide among the general population. And so, because the saints will not be able to purchase the food which they need to live, they will be forced out of society.

Luke 23:28-31 "But Jesus, turning to them, said, "Daughters of Jerusalem, do not weep for Me, but weep for yourselves and for your children. (29) For indeed the days are coming in which they will say, 'Blessed are the barren, wombs that never bore, and breasts which never nursed!' (30) Then they will begin 'to say to the mountains, "Fall on us!" and to the hills, "Cover us!" ' (31) For if they do these things in the green wood, what will be done in the dry?"

Summer is at the door

Our Lord Jesus made the above statement, as He was carrying His cross to Calvary. In context, our Lord was stating that if those in the world, could display such cruelty in His day, then how much more can we expect to see, when Satan and his cohorts have full reign in the earth. For our Lord said that, "if they do these things in the green wood, what will be done in the dry?" But we have also seen, that although it will be an extremely trying time for the saints in the earth, that the end of that three and half year period, will usher in the second coming of the Lord Jesus Christ.

The church is caught away

Luke 17:26-36 "And as it was in the days of Noah, so it will be also in the days of the Son of Man: (27) They ate, they drank, they married wives, they were given in marriage, until the day that Noah entered the ark, and the flood came and destroyed them all. (28) Likewise, as it was also in the days of Lot: They ate, they drank, they bought, they sold, they planted, they built; (29) but on the day that Lot went out of Sodom it rained fire and brimstone from heaven and destroyed them all. (30) Even so will it be in the day when the Son of Man is revealed. (31) "In that day, he who is on the housetop, and his goods are in the house, let him not come down to take them away. And likewise, the one who is in the field, let him not turn back. (32) Remember Lot's wife. (33) Whoever seeks to save his life will lose it, and whoever loses his life will preserve it. (34) I tell you, in that night there will be two in one bed: the one will be taken and the other will be left. (35) Two will be grinding together: the one will be taken and the other left. (36) Two will be in the field: the one will be taken and the other left."

In the above passage of scripture, our Lord Jesus described the event, of the catching away of His church, from the earth. As I mentioned in the previous section, although the church is appointed to tribulation, she is not appointed to wrath, and so she will not experience the wrath of God, that will be poured out on the earth, at the end of the age. In the above passage, our Lord tells us what the world will be like, just before the wrath of God is finally poured out on the earth, for He tells us that the world will be continuing with their daily lives, as normal. When our Lord teaches us this, He equates it to the times of Noah and Lot, for He tells us that their worlds also continued with life, blissfully unaware of their impending judgement. But when Noah and Lot were removed from those worlds, then sudden destruction came upon them. In the same manner, when the church is removed from the earth, sudden destruction will come upon all who are on the earth, and it will take them completely by surprise. The apostle Paul, confirms this truth to us by stating, "For when they say, "Peace and safety!" then sudden destruction comes upon them, as labour pains upon a pregnant woman. And they shall not escape" (1 Thessalonians 5:3). Our Lord went on in this passage, to describe the actual catching away of His church from the earth, and in His description, He gives us further insights into what it will be like for the saints, at that time. For I want you to notice, that He speaks of His saints, working in factories (grinding), and working in farmlands (in the field). And I also want you to notice, that He describes them as working alongside unbelievers. Clearly, not all saints in the earth at that time, will be experiencing intense persecution, for the saints that our Lord describes, will also be going about their daily lives, just as the rest of the unbelievers will. This point ties in with what we have said before, in that the Anti-Christ will only be able to persecute the saints, that find themselves in his kingdom. But we have also said, that the influence of his kingdom will spread during his reign, however, it will not have extended over the entire globe, before the church is caught away. Something else can be seen from this passage. When our Lord says that two will be in one bed, and the one will be taken and the other left, He is referring to married couples. And so, we see that as it is today, that one spouse believes while the other doesn't, so it will be at the end of the age. Just for clarity, I need to mention, that in this passage, when our Lord says, "In that day, he who is on the housetop, and his goods are in the house, let him not come down to take them away. And likewise, the one who is in the field, let him not turn back. Remember Lot's wife. Whoever seeks to save his life will lose it, and whoever loses his life will preserve it", He is referring to the outbreak of the great tribulation, and not the catching away of the church. For you will recall that we read earlier, where our Lord warned His church, to flee Judea at that time, and not go down to take anything out of his house. With regards to the catching away of the church, the scripture teaches us that we will be changed in the twinkling of an eye (1 Corinthians 15:52). In other words, there will be no time afforded to the believer, to pack their suitcase, before departing to meet the Lord in the air.

1 Corinthians 15:51-53 "Behold, I tell you a mystery: We shall not all sleep, but we shall all be changed-- (52) in a moment, in the twinkling of an eye, at the last trumpet. For the trumpet will sound, and the dead will be raised incorruptible, and we shall be changed. (53) For this corruptible must put on incorruption, and this mortal must put on immortality."

In the above passage of scripture, the Holy Spirit through the apostle Paul, also describes the event of the catching away of the church. In this passage, He tells us that not all Christians will taste death, for He says that not all shall sleep. The saints that will not physically die, are the saints that are alive on the earth, when our Lord Jesus returns to the earth. I will not go into the timeline of our Lord's second coming in any detail, as that falls outside the scope of this teaching, but let me mention that when our Lord returns, that He will not descend to the earth immediately. For the scripture teaches us, that we will meet Him, in the air. The "air", referred to in scripture, is the realm where Satan and his angels currently reside, for he is called the prince of the power of the air (Ephesians 2:2). As we saw earlier, Satan will no longer be in that realm, for Michael and his angels, would have already cast Satan and his angels, to the earth. It will be during our time, of being with our Lord in the air, that the church will be judged, by the Lord. And it is during that time, that the wrath of God, will be poured out on the earth. At the end of that period, we will descend to the earth with our Lord Jesus, and our Lord will begin His millennial reign on the earth. And so, we see that even though the scripture teaches us that it is appointed to men once to die, and after that the judgement (Hebrews 9:27), that God has made an exception in the saints that will be alive, when our Lord returns. We also see in this passage, that every saint will be changed, both those who are alive, and those who are dead, for those who are dead, will be raised from the dead. And from that moment on, the saints will become like angels, for they too will become immortal.

1 Thessalonians 4:15-17 "For this we say to you by the word of the Lord, that we who are alive and remain until the coming of the Lord will by no means precede those who are asleep. (16) For the Lord Himself will descend from heaven with a shout, with the voice of an archangel, and with the trumpet of God. And the dead in Christ will rise first. (17) Then we who are alive and remain shall be caught up together with them in the clouds to meet the Lord in the air. And thus, we shall always be with the Lord."

The same event of the catching away of the church, is described in the above passage of scripture. It is in this passage, that we see that we will meet our Lord Jesus in the air, as already mentioned. Let me say, that there is only one second coming of Christ, and that every saint (both Jews and Gentiles alike), will meet the Lord in the air, at His coming.

Revelation 8:1-6 "When He opened the seventh seal, there was silence in heaven for about half an hour. (2) And I saw the seven angels who stand before God, and to them were given seven trumpets. (3) Then another angel, having a golden censer, came and stood at the altar. He was given much incense, that he should offer it with the prayers of all the saints upon the golden altar which was before the throne. (4) And the smoke of the incense, with the prayers of the saints, ascended before God from the angel's hand. (5) Then the angel took the censer, filled it with fire from the altar, and threw it to the earth. And there were noises, thundering's, lightnings, and an earthquake. (6) So, the seven angels who had the seven trumpets prepared themselves to sound."

As I have already mentioned, it is when the church is caught away from the earth, that the wrath of God, will be poured out on those who remain on the earth. The above passage of scripture, describes the seven angels preparing themselves to sound their trumpets. If you read the book of Revelation, you will see that each of those trumpets, once sounded, reveals another judgement of God, poured out on the earth. This will be a horrific time, for those on the earth, but the church will not be present to experience it.

If you believe you can receive Jesus as your Lord and Saviour by praying this prayer

Dear Heavenly Father,

I come to You in the Name of Jesus.

Your Word says, "the one who comes to Me I will by no means cast out" (John 6:37), so I know You won't cast me out, but You take me in and I thank You for it. You said in Your Word, "Whoever calls on the name of the lord shall be saved." (Romans 10:13). I am calling on Your Name, so I know that You save me right now. You also said, "If you confess with your mouth the Lord Jesus and believe in your heart that God has raised Him from the dead, you will be saved. (10) For with the heart one believes unto righteousness, and with the mouth confession is made unto salvation" (Romans 10:9-10). I believe in my heart Jesus Christ is the Son of God. I believe that He was raised from the dead for my justification, and I confess Him now as my Lord. Because Your Word says, "with the heart one believes unto righteousness," and I do believe with my heart, I have now become the righteousness of God in Christ Jesus (2 Cor. 5:21) . . .

And I am now saved!

Thank You, Lord!

Welcome to the family of God. Now that you are His child you need to read your bible (especially the New

Testament) daily, spend time in prayer daily and join a local church that will teach you to be filled with the Holy Spirit with the evidence of speaking in other tongues, so that you can grow spiritually. You also need to tell others how Jesus has saved you so that they too can be saved.

About the Author

From childhood, Michael E.B. Maher has always known that the Lord's call was upon his life for the ministry. When he was saved at the age of twenty-two, almost immediately the Lord Jesus began to deal with him about entering the ministry. He went to Oral Roberts University to enrol but circumstances prevented him from following that path. After a period, the call for the ministry once again became very strong, and finally in the early 1990's Michael entered the ministry. After a period, he left the ministry and went into the business world. Although he experienced success in the business world, he was outside of the Lord's will for his life. Over time, he began to drift from the close relationship with the Lord that he had always known. By 2010 the Lord's patience had run out, and Michael suffered his first series of heart attacks. By this time, Michael had become so worldly in his thinking that it never even occurred to him that the Lord had begun to judge him for his disobedience. After his medical treatment, Michael went back into his career thinking that all was back on track again. But now the Lord started to unravel his career as well. Whereas before he had always excelled in his work, he now found completely dissatisfied with what he was doing. And so, at the height of his career he decided to take early retirement. It was during this time that his relationship with the Lord grew again. Although the Lord had brought him to this point, he was still not in the Lord's will. And so, Michael then had his next series of heart attacks. It was only now that the Lord finally got his attention and he committed to the Lord that if He would spare his life, that he would finally answer the Lord's call to the ministry.

And so, in 2014 Michael Maher Ministries was begun. From the beginning, the mandate given to Michael from the Lord Jesus was to preach the word. And so, this ministry preaches the word of God on every available platform around the world.

Michael Maher Ministries

Free Subscription

Join hundreds of others from countries around the world and read our Daily Bible Teaching Email and more, that will help you to grow in your walk with the Lord Jesus.

Thank you, sir, for helping me to understand these teachings clearly! Amen

> - *Tawanda Masvina*

Amen to keeping on keeping on. Thank you for today's lesson. We must never forget to pray regularly and immerse ourselves in the Word – "a page (or Chapter) a day helps keep Satan at bay".
Blessings,

> - *John Lombard*

Thank you so much for today's inspiration. This made so much sense to me and helped me overcome a huge block in my understanding.
Blessings and love

> - *Pam Laughton*

Log on to our website to subscribe.

www.mebmm.org

Michael Maher Ministries

Online Bible Courses

Our courses are designed to help believers grow in their faith and reach their full potential in Christ that God intended for their lives, through the study of His word.

Flexible

Enrol any time: choose your topic of study; study at your own pace.

Affordable

Pay as you go.

Log on to our website to register.

www.mebmm.org

Michael Maher Ministries

13 Windsor Lodge
Beach Road
Fish Hoek, 7974
Cape Town
South Africa
Phone: +27 082-974-3599

On the Web

www.mebmm.org

Notes

[1] From Wikipedia, Muslim population growth. Accessed November 21, 2017 through https://en.wikipedia.org/wiki/Muslim_population_growth

[2] From Joshua J. Mark (28 April 2011), Babylon. Accessed November 21, 2017 through https://www.ancient.eu/babylon/

[3] From ADL, Anti-Semitism in the US. Accessed November 21 2017 through https://www.adl.org/news/press-releases/us-anti-semitic-incidents-spike-86-percent-so-far-in-2017

[4] From Gili Cohen (10 October 2017), Middle East News. Accessed November 21, 2017 through https://www.haaretz.com/middle-east-news/1.816553

[5] From Carol Brooks, The Feasts of Israel. Accessed November 23, 2017 through http://www.inplainsite.org/html/seven_feasts_of_israel.html

[6] From Conservapedia, Orthodox Judaism. Accessed November 21, 2017 through http://www.conservapedia.com/Orthodox_Judaism

[7] From One for Israel, A Short History of Messianic Judaism. Accessed November 21, 2017 through https://www.oneforisrael.org/bible-based-teaching-from-israel/a-short-history-of-messianic-judaism/

[8] From Kelly James Clark, The Most Persecuted Religion in the World. Accessed November 21, 2017 through https://www.huffingtonpost.com/kelly-james-clark/christianity-most-persecuted-religion_b_2402644.html

[9] From Perry Chiaramonte (February 02, 2017), Christian persecution seen in more locations across the globe, new report shows. Accessed November 21, 2017 through http://www.foxnews.com/world/2017/02/02/christian-

persecution-seen-in-more-locations-across-globe-new-report-shows.html

[10] From Fareed Zakaria (June 20, 2016), Why they hate us. Accessed November 21, 2017 through http://edition.cnn.com/2016/04/08/opinions/why-they-hate-us-zakaria/index.html

[11] From Michael Rühle, Analysis - The nuclear dimensions of jihadist terrorism. Accessed November 21, 2017 through https://www.nato.int/docu/review/2007/Growing_Dangers/Nuclear_jihadist_terrorism/EN/index.htm

[12] From Beatrice Fihn (April 30, 2013), Remarks from RCW at NPT PrepCom side event on the humanitarian consequences of nuclear weapons. Accessed November 21, 2017 through http://www.reachingcriticalwill.org/resources/statements/7881-remarks-from-rcw-at-npt-prepcom-side-event-on-the-humanitarian-consequences-of-nuclear-weapons

[13] From Wikipedia, Mahdi. Accessed November 22, 2017 through https://en.wikipedia.org/wiki/Mahdi

[14] From Wikipedia, Messiah. Accessed November 22, 2017 through https://en.wikipedia.org/wiki/Messiah#Islam

[15] From Wikipedia, First Jewish–Roman War. Accessed November 22, 2017 through https://en.wikipedia.org/wiki/First_Jewish%E2%80%93Roman_War

[16] From Wikipedia, Pella, Jordan. Accessed November 22, 2017 through https://en.wikipedia.org/wiki/Pella,_Jordan

[17] From Wikipedia, Siege of Jerusalem (AD 70). Accessed November 22, 2017 through https://en.wikipedia.org/wiki/Siege_of_Jerusalem_(AD_70)